BILLY THE KID

BILLY THE KID

Beyond the Grave

W. C. Jameson

TAYLOR TRADE PUBLISHING
Dallas • Lanham • Boulder • New York • Toronto • Oxford

Published by Taylor Trade Publishing
An imprint of
The Rowman & Littlefield Publishing Group, Inc.
4501 Forbes Boulevard, Suite 200
Lanham, MD 20706

Distributed by NATIONAL BOOK NETWORK

Library of Congress Cataloging-in-Publication Data
Jameson, W. C., 1942–
Billy the Kid : beyond the grave / W. C. Jameson.
   p. cm.
Includes bibliographical references and index.
ISBN 1-58979-148-7 (cloth : alk. paper)
1. Billy, the Kid—Death and burial. 2. Roberts, William Henry, 1859–1950.
3. Outlaws—Southwest, New—Biography. 4. Impostors and imposture—United States—Case studies. 5. Southwest, New—Biography. I. Title. F786 .B54J355 2005
364.15'52'092—dc22

                                                        2004014244

To Max McCoy and Fred Bean,
the other two musketeers.

———◆◆◆———

Contents

◆◆◆

Foreword

❖❖❖

Quién es? Even now, one hundred and twenty-three years after history says these were Billy the Kid's last words before being sent to glory by Pat Garrett, the question lingers.

Who is it? Who was killed in Pete Maxwell's darkened bedroom on the night of July 14, 1881? Was it the Kid? Was he buried in the post cemetery at Fort Sumner, New Mexico? When the fort was abandoned and when the bodies of the soldiers buried there were eventually removed, were those remains relocated with the others to Santa Fe? Or did Billy the Kid really survive the midnight ambush, as author W. C. Jameson suggests, only to die of natural causes a few days before his ninety-first birthday in 1950? And does it even matter, after all these years?

Of course it does. Billy the Kid is an authentic American icon—much to the consternation of generations of historians, moralizers, and other assorted killjoys. Ask any schoolboy or schoolgirl to name the twentieth president of the United States, and you're likely to get a blank stare. But ask about Billy the Kid, and he or she will correctly identify an outlaw; you might even get that old chestnut about Billy's killing a man for each of his twenty-one years. Twentieth president James A. Garfield, by the way, was shot by a bloodthirsty attorney the same month in 1881 that history says the Kid found his bullet. Garfield, however, lingered until September. For your name to be more widely known than the contemporary president is not bad for a teenaged outlaw whose only authentic surviving photograph shows a rather goofy-looking young man with a crooked grin, a big hat, and an even bigger gun. To be fair, however, those who knew the Kid—especially the women—swore the tintype simply did not do Billy justice.

Folklorists have a rather easier time with Billy than do historians because the former, like children, recognize the need for heroes in popular American tradition. And because of a complicated legacy that includes Anglo-Saxon hero worship going back at least to Robin Hood, we just can't get enough of outlaws. Jesse James and Billy the Kid were not really heroes, but they have been elevated to the same cult status as Sir Robin of Locksley. All were proficient with weapons; all were said to fight for the rich and give to the poor, or at least fight on the side of right; and all were betrayed by those they trusted. Even more curious, all are said to really have never died at all, or at least not in the way history records. Most, it is said, lived to secretly enjoy a ripe old age. Similar stories are told about just about every old West outlaw of any note, including Butch Cassidy, and of the outlaws of our day—rock-and-roll stars such as Elvis and Jim Morrison.

The dime novels made a fortune trading in Billy's legend, and even Pat Garrett cashed in with a book purporting to tell the Kid's "authentic" life—which was full of lies. More recently, at least fifty major films have been made about the Kid, with stars such as Kris Kristofferson and Val Kilmer in the leading roles. Composer Aaron Copland and singer–songwriter Bob Dylan have contributed music for the legend, while writers of no less stature than Michael Ondaatje and Gore Vidal have tackled what the Kid's legacy really means to us.

Still, even with the millions of words and images and notes that have seeped into the popular culture in these 123 years, the question remains: Who *was* he? This book attempts to provide an answer.

Read it with an open mind. Follow the detective story that Jameson expertly tells, beginning with a mysterious trunk and a set of old reel-to-reel tapes that turn to dust even as Austin writer Fred Bean frantically attempts to transcribe them. Pay attention to what the experts have to say about the photographic evidence. And when you're done, judge for yourself. I'll wager that you'll think maybe—just maybe—that William Henry Roberts really was Billy the Kid. At the very least, you'll keep asking yourself: *¿Quién es?*

Max McCoy, author of *Indiana Jones and
the Secret of the Sphinx*; *Jesse: A Novel of the
Outlaw Jesse James*; and *The Moon Pool*

Preface:
The "Death" of Billy the Kid
◆◆◆

Near midnight, July 14, 1881, a young man, shirtless and in stockinged feet, pads softly across hard-packed ground in a moonlit courtyard. His destination is a supply storeroom and a freshly butchered carcass of beef. One hand holds a long-bladed knife. A moment before stepping onto wooden porch planks under a roofed walkway, he is spotted by two deputy sheriffs, John Poe and Thomas McKinney. Both shift their hands to their pistol grips, wary eyes focusing on the silent newcomer.

Poe and McKinney, already concerned about creeping onto the property with sheriff Pat Garrett, are keenly aware they are outnumbered should the Mexican residents of Pete Maxwell's Fort Sumner ranch become hostile to their presence. Their quarry, Billy the Kid—killer, cattle rustler, and veteran of the Lincoln County War—is friend to all here and is held in high regard by men and women alike. Most would rise up against any who would threaten him.

As the stranger approaches, he detects a slight movement from the direction of Poe and McKinney. Not expecting anyone to be out this time of night, he advances with caution.

¿Quién es? ¿Quién es? he whispers in Spanish. (Who is it? Who is it?)

Poe and McKinney eye the approaching figure with suspicion. Only seconds earlier, Sheriff Garrett had entered the bedroom of rancher Pete Maxwell to speak with him regarding the whereabouts of the outlaw Billy the Kid. The open doorway lies just a few feet beyond the deputies. As the shoeless man walks past Poe, he hears muffled conversation coming from the room. Stepping inside the doorway, he whispers again, *¿Quién es?*

Sudden movement near the rear wall catches his attention, and he peers into the darkness. Seeing Maxwell rise to a seated position on the bed, he is about to speak again when a gunshot explodes, then another. Knocked backward from the impact of a bullet, the young man drops his knife and collapses to the floor near the open doorway, blood oozing from a wound in his chest. From behind a bed, a shaken Pat Garrett rises to his full height and takes one cautious step toward the prone, somewhat frail-looking body on Maxwell's floor. Then, he turns and dashes out the doorway to find Poe and McKinney waiting.

"Boys," the sheriff exhales, "that was the Kid, and I think I have got him." Then, Garrett slumps against the outer wall. Deputy Poe peers into the doorway to gaze at the lifeless form on the floor. "Pat," he says, "the Kid would not come to this place; you have shot the wrong man." Garrett stiffens. A vain, image-conscious sheriff with political ambitions, he reacts quickly. "I am sure that was him, for I know his voice too well to be mistaken."

Awakened by the gunshots, Fort Sumner residents fill the court-yard. Garrett orders Poe and McKinney to close the door to Maxwell's bedroom. No one, he tells the two deputies, is allowed to enter except under orders. Within minutes, what would become one of the biggest controversies in the history of the American West is born: the death of the outlaw Billy the Kid.

Garrett locks himself in the room with the corpse while Poe and McKinney stand guard outside, rifles ready, facing a growing throng of Fort Sumner residents. Throughout the crowd, word is carried that Garrett claimed to have killed their friend Billy the Kid. Whispered conversations, however, echo Deputy Poe's initial observation: Pat Garrett killed the wrong man, and Billy the Kid lives!

Hours later, as dawn illuminates the porch where the two deputies stand guard, even more curious events are about to unfold—the mysterious inquest and burial of the man Pat Garrett claimed was Billy the Kid.

Acknowledgments

Thanks to the late Fred Bean for his friendship, his personal files, his contributions to this project, and for sharing his passion for adventure; to the late Dr. C. L. Sonnichsen for his insight, patience, scholarship, professionalism, and great conversations we shared; to the late Bill Allison for turning over to us the wooden trunk filled with evidence, taped conversations, letters, notes, transcriptions, and photographs; to Drs. Alan Bovik and Scott Acton and the University of Texas at Austin; to Judge Andre McNeil and attorney Helen Rice Grinder for examining and evaluating the evidence; to Howard Chandler for the handwriting analysis; to Dr. James M. Thompson for his medical expertise; to Marguerite Thomas for helping tie up loose ends; to Laurie Wagner Buyer for her encouragement, guidance, and inspiration; and to Janet Harris for her editorial mastery and keeping me on track.

I am indebted to the following institutions, agencies, and individuals for their help in locating and providing important papers, documents, and photographs: the Indiana Historical Collection and William Henry Smith Memorial Library, Indianapolis; the Rio Grande Historical Collection, New Mexico State University Library, Las Cruces; the Nita Stewart Haley Memorial Library, Midland, Texas; the Western History Collection, University of Oklahoma, Norman; Christine Leischow and Special Collections, University of Arizona, Tucson; and Kathleen Ferris and the Center for Southwest Research, University of New Mexico, Albuquerque.

ONE

◆◆◆

Pat Garrett Killed the Wrong Man

More than a century has passed since the alleged killing of the outlaw Billy the Kid. Regardless of which position a researcher assumes on the matter, absolute proof of what actually occurred that night in 1881, what transpired during the days leading up to it, and the subsequent inquest and burial does not exist. Despite what most history books contend, there is a strong possibility that the outlaw known as Billy the Kid was not shot by sheriff Pat Garrett on the night of July 14, 1881, in Fort Sumner, New Mexico.

The notion that the Kid was killed, one supported by some legitimate historians as well as a host of lawmen and outlaw enthusiasts, relies on evidence that does not hold up under thorough, logical analysis. The greatest portion of this evidence is based on the word of Pat Garrett as presented in his book *The Authentic Life of Billy the Kid*, a book that has been characterized by researchers such as Frederick Nolan and Leon Metz as filled with errors, misinterpretations, and blatant lies.

Conversely, the evidence that Billy the Kid survived that dark night in Fort Sumner and went on to live a long, though not necessarily happy, life is plentiful, provocative, and compelling. One important part of it is based on science—a statistically significant photo comparison employed by the world's foremost law enforcement agencies—and rigorous research that uncovered overlooked and ignored information. This evidence leads to conclusions that depart dramatically from the historical status quo, which is based largely on the discredited word of Pat Garrett.

Curious and captivating evidence exists to support the notion that the famous outlaw may have survived for nearly seven decades following his reported death at the hands of Garrett. A quiet, elderly man living under an alias in a small Texas town was discovered accidentally by a paralegal case worker during the routine handling of an estate settlement in 1948. Armed with information obtained from an acquaintance of the man, the paralegal asked if he was, in fact, the outlaw known as Billy the Kid. The old man initially denied it, admitting only his real name—William Henry Roberts.

Throughout the years, a number of scholars, writers, and observers have generally agreed that few aspects of America's history have captured the attention and imagination of the public as much as the myriad collection of images and events associated with the nation's Wild West era. The indelible images generated during these wondrous, fascinating, boisterous, unsettled, colorful, and active years more than a century ago have been recorded, glorified, studied, novelized, reenacted in film and on stage, captured in song, and absorbed one way or another into the collective consciousness of most Americans as well as millions more in Europe and Asia. There is no denying the romance and attraction of Western-period events such as the trail-drive days, when great herds of Texas longhorns were driven to the railheads in faraway plains such as Abilene and Dodge City, Kansas; and Omaha and North Platte, Nebraska. Compelling and profound is the impact made by the herder of that time, that uniquely North American figure so often reincarnated in the form of the enduring and noble figure of the American cowboy. This figure has transcended imagery to the point of becoming representative of nearly all that is Western. The mythical cowboy icon is nothing if not versatile. It comes in limitless shapes, forms, colors, ethnic backgrounds, qualities, and editions; and each holds some appeal to various elements of American culture and society.

One common image is that of the loner, the man of unknown origins who rode about the Western landscape working occasional trail drives or ranch jobs. This figure has been a common fare of novels for decades and in film, aptly represented by Alan Ladd's character in *Shane* and that of Clint Eastwood's man-with-no-name role in a variety of spaghetti Westerns. Accompanied by little more than his horse and gun, the cowboy, at least in novels and film, could be counted on for such heroics as helping out damsels in distress, saving a ranch from a greedy banker, routing gangs of rustlers and train robbers, or simply exacting revenge when needed.

These images, with others, come and go now as much as they did in the past. Another figure from those times that has remained constant, however, is that of the outlaw. He is called by other names—highwayman, brigand, bandit, desperado, gunman—but the outlaw of the American West has long been, and continues to be, one of the world's most enduring icons.

Why such an image should remain so persistent and pervasive is often debated, but one sentiment agreed on by most relates to the notion that Americans and others seem to need renegades. This has been explained in a number of ways, but most agree that the Western outlaw is an unusual package consisting of a variety of elements, many of which happen to be quite appealing.

The outlaw is a man chased after and persecuted by authorities. His response is frequently interpreted as an expression of defiance, of standing up against his oppressors, political and economic. The outlaw is often characterized as fighting for his perceived rights. He is generally viewed as being free-spirited and rebellious; and Americans, as well as others, like to identify with that. Thanks to novels and films, the Western outlaw has evolved into a romantic figure, often cloaked in mystery and possessing a certain roguish charm. The outlaw has become a celebrity and folk hero. When Americans are asked to identify notable figures from the nation's past, many will name outlaws such as Billy the Kid and Jesse James.

In his book *The Great American Outlaw: A Legacy of Fact and Fiction*, author Frank Richard Prassel says the great American outlaw is a legendary figure shrouded in myth and that his "stories are legends passed from generation to generation, retold as truth, and reflecting people's needs and hopes." Prassel notes that these tales often have suppressed meanings and long-forgotten origins and that they are not unique to the United States—that "every culture includes countless assertions, endlessly recounted until they become versions of reality which are actually constructions of miscommunication." "Myth," says Prassel, "may thus emerge as substantive parts of social history capable of influencing present concepts and courses of action with consequences both good and bad."

Tales of outlaws in virtually all cultures are suitable to this process because "the lives of fugitives abound with gaps and confusion," Prassel observes. Imaginative bits and pieces taken from other stories often conveniently complete a desired picture with contradiction and easily detected errors coexisting with a few leading facts. When this is supplemented by popular novels and motion pictures, "These legends may be further transformed into cultural institutions."

Prassell is describing the prevailing perceptions of the outlaw Billy the Kid. Scholars and hobbyists alike, however pure their motives, are responsible for clouding the image of the Kid; they have recorded legend and lore and presented it as historical fact.

Prominent American outlaw figures such as Jesse James, Butch Cassidy, Belle Starr, the Daltons, the Youngers, and Billy the Kid are best known in their fictional and mythic forms, not their true historic ones. These figures are loved and in many ways idolized, cherished, and valued.

Several of America's outlaws were and are so compelling and appealing in that they cannot die, even when they have apparently been killed. Deeply etched into the consciousness, these enigmatic personalities remained alive in story, song, and film. Society seems to nurture its favorite outlaw heroes, adding to their exploits over time, polishing the luster afforded them by earlier generations. Whether England's Robin Hood was a real person or a fictional one has never been entirely clear, but his outlaw persona has endured for more than six hundred years. From time to time, one or another of the more famous outlaws appears to return from his alleged demise, showing up years later.

During the past century, dozens of men have come forth claiming to be the outlaw Jesse James, to have survived the cowardly shooting by Robert Ford in 1882. The most notable of these claimants was a man named J. Frank Dalton, who lived well into his eighties. While questions still surround the death of James, none of the claimants, including Dalton, ever presented a coherent and defensible case for his identity.

Likewise, many are convinced that the outlaw Butch Cassidy was not killed by soldiers in South America and that he returned to the United States and lived a long life among friends someplace in the West. The evidence that Cassidy was gunned down in a hail of bullets contains many loose ends consisting of conjecture and lore. However, the claim that the outlaw lived and returned to the United States was supported by a number of credible witnesses, including old friends and relatives who allegedly spent time with him following his reappearance.

A preponderance of evidence exists that John Wilkes Booth, the assassin of President Abraham Lincoln, was not killed in a burning barn in Virginia in 1865 but escaped to live for at least another thirty-five years. Though more than two dozen men have claimed to be Booth, the one who received the most publicity was a man who went by the aliases John St. Helen and David E. George. George confessed to an attorney that he was the famous assassin and that he had lived his life in hiding, corresponding occasionally with members of his famous family of actors.

Few of the claimants associated with these personalities were ever taken seriously. Though the evidence presented was often intriguing and provocative, subsequent investigation yielded little that could be considered supportive. In the cases of John Wilkes Booth and Butch Cassidy, the claims for their survival and return were advanced not by the principals themselves but by others who stumbled onto their identities.

British writer Frederick Nolan says that Billy the Kid is "the most popular and enduring legend in American folklore." As his fame grew and as his folkloric image endured and prospered since his alleged death at the hands of Garrett in 1881, the outlaw Billy the Kid may have been alive and in hiding. After being discovered by paralegal William V. Morrison in 1948, William Henry Roberts was unable to keep his secret. He had the look, the size, the features, and the scars. In addition, and perhaps more important, he knew too much. At the time of his discovery and during subsequent interviews, Roberts manifested an impressive and intimate knowledge of New Mexico's Lincoln County War and its associated personalities and politics during the 1870s and 1880s, a knowledge that exceeded that of the historians of the day. This is significant because Roberts was illiterate and barely able to read and write. Confronted with substantial evidence by the persistent paralegal, Roberts broke down. In tears, he admitted he had been running and hiding from the law for most of his life and confessed his true identity—the outlaw Billy the Kid. Noted historian, folklorist, and writer C. L. Sonnichsen described Roberts as a "Western Lazarus, risen from the dead with a six-shooter in each hand, who was willing to tell of his experiences behind the veil."

This revelation, with subsequent press coverage orchestrated by the paralegal, thrust Roberts into the headlines of the day. The idea that he could be Billy the Kid ignited a controversy that persists into the twenty-first century. The claim was basically rejected outright, particularly by those faithful to the long-accepted history that maintains the Kid was killed by sheriff Pat Garrett in 1881. How could a man as notorious as Billy the Kid, an outlaw with an extremely high profile as a result of dime novels and film, remain hidden for seven decades?

Undaunted, Morrison was determined to conduct research into the background of Roberts, and he worked diligently to procure and provide evidence that the old man could be Billy the Kid. The well-intentioned Morrison was unfortunately not an experienced or qualified researcher. While he made some surprising discoveries, his attempts were unschooled. To further complicate the situation, Morrison intended to propel himself into the limelight with his discovery, in hopes of fame and money. Morrison made numerous mistakes, and his uncompromising manner alienated many who might have been sympathetic to his aims. Morrison, in fact, became a target for the critics almost as much as Roberts was.

After Morrison's initial investigations of Roberts during the late 1940s, little substantive research was conducted. For decades, many remained intrigued by the notion that William Henry Roberts could have been the famous outlaw Billy the Kid. Nagging doubts raised by the questionable accuracy of the recorded history of the Kid and the Lincoln County War refused to go away. The more Pat Garrett is studied and analyzed, the easier it is to conclude he was as much a promoter and prevaricator as lawman. Conversely, the more William Henry Roberts is objectively examined, the more his veracity and credibility seem greater than Garrett's.

During the late 1980s, Frederic Bean, noted author of forty novels, became acquainted with Roberts's stepgrandson Bill Allison. Nearly eighty years old, Allison contacted Bean and said he was interested in "getting out the truth about Roberts." Allison provided Bean with an old wooden trunk that had belonged to Roberts. The trunk contained several reels of taped conversations between Roberts and Morrison and copies of letters from Morrison to Roberts and others, including noted historians of the day. There were other items in the trunk that verified Roberts's accounts and substantiated claims that Roberts was the outlaw Billy the Kid.

Bean's discoveries, the findings of other researchers, and a scientific photo-comparison analysis resulted in important revelations regarding Roberts. This substantive evidence contradicted much of the traditional history of Billy the Kid that had been unconditionally accepted by nearly everyone who encountered it.

TWO

A Traditional History
of the Outlaw Billy the Kid

The young outlaw known as Billy the Kid was little different from other small-time bad men of his day. In many ways, he was a run-of-the-mill, hard-luck cattle rustler, no more or no less colorful or noteworthy than most of his companions.

Despite that, Billy the Kid entered Western legend a short time after his alleged death at the hands of sheriff Pat Garrett, and there he remains, more than a century later. There are two principal reasons for this. Dime novels regaled readers with the adventures and heroics of authentic and made-up characters of the Wild West. Novelists either colored the truth or ignored it altogether. They often manufactured events to keep the excitement level high and the plot moving. A number of these books wildly exaggerated Billy the Kid's misdeeds, such as killing twenty-one men and burying a wooden chest filled with treasure.

About a year after allegedly killing Billy the Kid, Pat Garrett authored a book titled *The Authentic Life of Billy the Kid, the Noted Desperado of the Southwest, Whose Deeds of Daring and Blood Have Made His Name a Terror in New Mexico, Arizona and Northern Mexico, by Pat F. Garrett, Sheriff of Lincoln County, N. Mex., by Whom He Was Finally Hunted Down and Captured by Killing Him.* The publication is known today simply as *The Authentic Life of Billy the Kid.* The book, mostly written by Garrett's friend Marshall Ashmun Upson, had much in common with the dime novels in that it contained very little truth and a great deal of fiction.

Writer Frederick Nolan annotated and wrote an introduction for the University of Oklahoma Press reprint of Garrett's *The Authentic Life of Billy the Kid* (2000). Nolan refers to the book as "a farrago of nonsense" that "has been responsible for every single one of the myths

perpetuated about Billy the Kid" and for "many inaccuracies, eva-
sions, and even untruths."

Unfortunately, most of what the public knows, or thinks· they
know, about Billy the Kid is derived from this book, an outrageous
collection of misinformation and fabrication. In the years following
the publication of *Authentic Life*, hundreds, if not thousands, of
subsequent books, articles, pamphlets, and films perpetuated the
mistaken notions originally generated by the Garrett–Upson exag-
gerations and lies.

During the years since the Garrett shooting, there has evolved a
"history" of Billy the Kid that gained a level of acceptance among historians, history buffs, and writers who have relied on one another's
research and published works. As a result, there emerged a tacit
agreement on a history of the Kid, including bits and pieces of a contrived genealogy, a chronology of his geographic wanderings, his involvement in the Lincoln County War, his arrests, his escapes, the
number of men he killed, and his death. The biography, in one form
or another, eventually became the standard found in nearly every
published book and film on the life of Billy the Kid.

Billy the Kid was born illegitimate in New York City on November
23, 1859, to Catherine McCarthy, an Irish immigrant. He was
named Henry and had an older brother, Joseph. Their father was
believed to be a man named Edward McCarthy, a peddler who already had a wife.

When Henry was about fourteen years of age, he was sent by the
New York Children's Aid Society to live with William Antrim. Brother
Joseph arrived later, and not long afterward Antrim married the
mother, Catherine, on March 1, 1873, in Santa Fe, New Mexico. After
drifting around New Mexico for a time, the family settled in Silver
City, where Catherine died from consumption.

In Silver City, young Henry first encountered trouble. He and a
friend stole some garments from a Chinese laundry, were captured,
and sent to jail. Henry escaped by crawling up a chimney.

At seventeen or eighteen years of age, Henry traveled to Camp
Grant, Arizona, near Tucson. At Camp Grant, Henry Antrim, as he
was now calling himself, had a fatal encounter with Frank P. "Windy"
Cahill. Following some name-calling, the two men began struggling,
and during the fight Henry pulled a pistol and shot Cahill through the
stomach. As Cahill lay dying, Henry was arrested. Days later, however, he escaped and fled back to New Mexico, where he began calling

himself William Bonney and then later, Billy the Kid. After drifting for weeks, he arrived in Seven Rivers, New Mexico, in October 1877, where he found a job on the Jones Ranch.

Later, Billy worked for an Englishman, John Tunstall. The cattleman and entrepreneur was competing for trade with Lawrence G. Murphy, a retired military officer. Murphy, with partners Jimmy Dolan and Emil Fritz, ran a general store in Lincoln and held a contract to sell beef to the military. Deciding to try to break Murphy's business monopoly, Tunstall opened a store and bank in the town of Lincoln and formed a partnership with a lawyer named Alexander McSween.

Murphy also controlled Lincoln County sheriff William Brady and employed a gang of toughs led by Jesse Evans, a rustler who also had a reputation as a gunman. At one point, Murphy retained McSween to collect on a $10,000 life insurance policy on partner Fritz, who died during a trip to Germany. McSween collected the money but refused to hand it over to Murphy. Under orders from Murphy, Sheriff Brady attempted to seize some of Tunstall's cattle as partial payment.

Tunstall decided he needed to confer with Brady, and he arranged to meet him in Lincoln. On February 18, 1878, John Tunstall, driving a buckboard and accompanied by several of his own hired hands, including Billy the Kid, set out for Lincoln. As they approached the town of Ruidoso, the riders spotted a flock of turkeys and set off in pursuit. Seconds later, a party of men led by Jesse Evans rode up to Tunstall and shot him dead, thus starting what came to be called the Lincoln County War.

Tunstall's hired hands vowed vengeance and organized themselves into a vigilante group. Under the leadership of Dick Brewer, they called themselves the Regulators. About three weeks following the death of Tunstall, the Regulators encountered Frank Baker and William Morton, two members of the party responsible for the killing. Baker and Morton were captured and then, according to the Regulators, shot while they were trying to escape.

On April 1, the Regulators rode into the town of Lincoln determined to gain even more vengeance. Seven of them, including Billy the Kid, were hiding behind a fence at Tunstall's store when Sheriff Brady, accompanied by deputy George Hindman, county clerk Billy Mathews, John Long, and George Peppin came walking down the street.

When they were within range, the Regulators opened fire on them, killing Brady and Hindman. After coming out from behind the fence,

Billy the Kid was wounded in the leg by Mathews, who fired from a place of concealment.

The killing of Brady and Hindman aroused the ire of many area residents, and the Regulators sought sanctuary at Blazer's Mill. Three days after the shooting, one of the men spotted Andrew "Buckshot" Roberts approaching the mill along the road. Roberts, another member of the gang that gunned down Tunstall, was unaware of the presence of the Regulators. A gunfight erupted, resulting in the death of Roberts and Tunstall's foreman, Dick Brewer, as well as the wounding of George Coe. Billy the Kid suffered a light flesh wound in the arm.

While lawyer Alexander McSween oversaw the late Tunstall's businesses, George Peppin was appointed sheriff of Lincoln County, to succeed Brady. Jimmy Dolan assumed control of Murphy's enterprises when Murphy died. Dolan believed he had the right, as well as the firepower, to run McSween out of town and shut down his businesses. McSween learned of Dolan's intentions and surrounded himself with the Regulators in his barricaded Lincoln home, awaiting attack.

Sheriff Peppin requested McSween's surrender, but the lawyer, feeling secure with the Regulators, refused. A five-day gun battle ensued, one that eventually involved soldiers from nearby Fort Stanton. On the night of July 19, one of Peppin's deputies set fire to McSween's house, forcing the occupants to flee. As he stepped out of the burning structure, McSween was shot and killed. Billy the Kid, assuming leadership of the Regulators, escaped. With the killing of McSween, the Lincoln County War was over.

During February 1879, Billy the Kid had a chance meeting with his old adversary Jesse Evans, and the two men decided to set their differences aside. While the Kid, Evans, and Dolan conferred on a street in Lincoln, an attorney named Huston Chapman happened by. Chapman had been employed by McSween's widow to prosecute members of the Dolan faction for murdering her husband. An argument erupted between Chapman and Evans. As the Kid took a couple of steps away from the scene, Evans and Dolan shot Chapman, poured liquor onto his clothes, and set him afire.

Lew Wallace, the new governor of New Mexico, later the author of the novel *Ben Hur*, was disturbed by questionable Murphy–Dolan beef contracts as well as by the murder of Chapman. In response to correspondence from the Kid, Wallace agreed to meet with him in Lincoln. Wallace, who wanted to break up what he considered a corrupt faction, promised the Kid that if he would testify against Dolan, he would not be prosecuted for the killing of Sheriff Brady. The Kid agreed, and on April 14 he provided testimony that resulted in Evans and Dolan's being indicted for Chapman's murder.

District attorney William R. Rynerson, however, was a Dolan supporter. After letting Dolan and Evans go, he ordered the Kid confined to jail. Though Billy the Kid wrote letters to Governor Wallace reminding him of his promise of amnesty, the Kid remained a prisoner. At the first opportunity, he escaped. In January 1880, he shot and killed Joe Grant during an argument in a Fort Sumner saloon.

In Lincoln, Pat Garrett ran for the office of sheriff on the promise that he would restore law and order to the region. After winning the election in November, he set about tracking down Billy the Kid. The Kid was reportedly hanging around White Oaks and behaving boisterously. A posse learned of his presence there and pursued him to the Greathouse Ranch. While the Kid and his companions sought refuge in the ranch house, a party of lawmen surrounded the place and demanded their surrender. When the standoff grew tiresome, deputy James Carlyle entered the ranch house to confer with the Kid. Billy immediately took him prisoner. In response, a posse member sent a message stating that unless Carlyle was released, a hostage would be killed. Moments later a shot was fired, and Carlyle, apparently convinced the hostage had been executed, tried to escape by jumping out of the nearest window and was immediately cut down by gunfire, believed by many to have come from the ranch house. Days later, Governor Wallace announced a five-hundred-dollar reward for Billy the Kid.

Billy and his small gang fled to Fort Sumner, where they were convinced they would be safe. Garrett, on learning of the Kid's presence in that settlement, decided to go after him. While the sheriff and several deputies hid in an abandoned hospital building near town, the Kid and his gang were spotted riding up the road. When the riders were close enough, the lawmen opened fire, mortally wounding Tom O'Folliard. The rest of the gang escaped.

Garrett's posse tracked the outlaws, cornering them in a rock house near Stinking Springs. In silence, they surrounded the structure during the night. At dawn, a man Garrett mistook for Billy the Kid exited the rock house, and the sheriff gave the order to fire. Billy's good friend Charlie Bowdre, unarmed, was struck several times and started bleeding badly. He staggered back into the house. Billy placed a revolver in Bowdre's hand and shoved the dying man back outside, telling him to go kill some of the attackers. Bowdre stumbled only a few steps from the door before he collapsed and died. A short time later, Billy and the remaining gang members surrendered and were sent to jail in Santa Fe. From his cell, the Kid dictated letters to Governor Wallace but received no response.

On March 28, the Kid was transported to Mesilla to stand trial for the killing of Sheriff Brady. On April 26, a jury returned a verdict of guilty. The judge, Warren Bristol, another Murphy–Dolan man, ordered Billy the Kid to be returned to Lincoln and hanged.

Back in Lincoln, the Kid was chained to the second floor of the old Murphy–Dolan store, which now served as a courthouse and jail. Garrett, who was out collecting taxes, assigned deputies J. W. Bell and Robert Olinger to guard the Kid.

Olinger, a large, burly man who had earned the reputation of a bully, constantly taunted and threatened the Kid. On the afternoon of April 28, Olinger escorted a small contingent of prisoners across the street to eat lunch at the Wortley Hotel. Before leaving the jail, he placed his shotgun in a cabinet in a confinement area. Once alone with Deputy Bell, the Kid requested that he be allowed to use the outhouse at the rear of the building. Inside the privy, the Kid located a pistol believed to have been left for him. He stuffed it inside his shirt. While being returned to the jail, the Kid paused at the head of the steps, pulled the pistol, and pointed it at Bell. The deputy immediately turned and fled back down the stairs, the Kid shooting at him as he ran. A few steps into the yard, Bell collapsed and died from a wound.

On hearing the shots, Deputy Olinger left the restaurant. As he returned to the courthouse, the Kid pulled the shotgun from the cabinet and moved to a window overlooking the northeast corner of the building. As Olinger approached, the Kid cut him down with two blasts from the deputy's own shotgun.

Obtaining a pickax from jail cook Godfrey Gauss, the Kid hammered at his leg irons, finally breaking one open. He then rode out of town and sought refuge at Pete Maxwell's place in Fort Sumner. Maxwell had known the Kid but was bothered by the outlaw's affection for his servant girls. Maxwell sent word to Garrett.

On the night of July 14, 1881, the Kid was visiting with Celsa Gutierrez, one of Maxwell's hired girls. When he mentioned that he was hungry, Celsa told Billy that Maxwell had that very day hung a portion of freshly butchered steer on his porch. The Kid, shirtless and in his stockinged feet, grabbed a knife and walked toward Maxwell's residence.

As he stepped onto the porch, the Kid spotted deputies Thomas McKinney and John Poe lurking in the dark. Neither of them recognized the Kid and presumed the newcomer was a friend of Maxwell's. Curious as to the identity of the men on the porch and unaware that Garrett was in the room with Maxwell, the Kid stepped into the rancher's quarters whispering *¿Quién es? ¿Quién es?* (Who is it? Who is it?)

Seconds later, the pistol of Pat Garrett boomed twice, and Billy the Kid, mortally wounded, collapsed to the floor, dead.

THREE

✦✦✦

The Discovery of
William Henry Roberts

Within hours after the shooting in Pete Maxwell's bedroom, Fort Sumner's Mexican residents whispered that the dead man was not Billy the Kid. According to some, the Kid had escaped and was in hiding not far away at the home of a friend.

Despite the assertions of Pat Garrett, there remained a strong belief that the Kid was not the man killed by the sheriff and that the young outlaw had fled to Mexico. For decades, the tale that the Kid was still alive was commonly heard throughout the Texas and New Mexico Southwest. The notion that Billy survived became attractive to a growing number of people, and it gave those who found the boy outlaw a romantic and enduring figure much to consider.

For years following the shooting, a number of men came forward claiming to be the Kid. Attention and notoriety for these claimants was generally short-lived, for subsequent investigations proved them to be imposters. One who received some attention was an old cowboy who lived in Ramah, New Mexico, and called himself John Miller. During the last few years of his life and for many years following his death, Miller's adopted son and some friends insisted he was Billy the Kid. The only evidence they offered, however, was that Miller had told them so.

By contrast, one particular man who had some intimate and confounding connections with the Lincoln County War remained in relative obscurity for sixty-seven years. After decades of living in Mexico, Texas, Arkansas, and Oklahoma, William Henry Roberts, with his wife, Melinda, settled into a life of semiretirement in central Texas during the 1940s.

After leaving New Mexico in 1881, Roberts spent most of the rest of his life earning a living at what he knew—livestock. He worked as a cowhand, earned an impressive reputation as a breaker of horses, bought and sold livestock, ran his own cattle and horse ranches on occasion, worked for the Wild West shows of Buffalo Bill and Pawnee Bill, and later operated a Wild West show of his own. In addition, Roberts, as many former outlaws, found employment in law enforcement, serving time with the Pinkertons, the U.S. marshal force, and as a city policeman. During this time, Roberts never used his real name, only aliases.

By the time he reached his eighties, Roberts's income amounted to only the paltry sum he received from welfare and what Melinda earned from taking in washing. When Roberts arrived at an age where he was no longer able to work, he resided in places where the low cost of living helped to stretch the meager family income. In search of one such place, he found Hamilton County, Texas.

Now and then, Roberts encountered old-timers, veterans from the Lincoln County War who remembered him as a participant during that long ago time and recognized him as the outlaw Billy the Kid. Unless he was with close friends, however, the old man denied the identity and found reason to excuse himself from further conversation.

During the late 1940s, a man named William V. Morrison was employed part-time by a law firm to conduct investigatory work relative to wills, deeds, inheritance claims, and related matters. Morrison found satisfaction as well as extra income from putting his paralegal skills to good use in the office and field.

A member of the Missouri Historical Society, Morrison enjoyed reading and researching history when time permitted. He claimed to be a descendant of Ferdinand Maxwell, the brother of Lucien Bonaparte Maxwell and uncle of Pete Maxwell, in whose bedroom Billy the Kid was supposedly shot and killed by Pat Garrett. Morrison, familiar with aspects of New Mexico history, had a passing knowledge of the Lincoln County War.

In 1948, Morrison's employer, a legal firm in Beaumont, Texas, sent him to Florida to investigate the case of Joe Hines, whose brother passed away in North Dakota. The elderly Florida resident claimed to be the sole inheritor of some property left by the relative. While interviewing the old man, Morrison learned that the name Joe Hines was an alias, a fact that caused some difficulty for processing the inheritance claim.

Another piece of information revealed to Morrison during the interview, one that would take on great importance, was that Hines admitted to participating in the Lincoln County War and stated that he fought against Billy the Kid. Though it has never been proven, some researchers believe that Morrison's personal notes from this interview indicated that the old man named Hines was, in reality, Jesse Evans. Proud of his knowledge of New Mexico history, Morrison told Hines of his ancestral connection and made an offhand comment about Billy the Kid's being gunned down by Garrett in the bedroom of Pete Maxwell.

To Morrison's utter surprise, Hines leaned close and told him that Garrett did not kill the Kid and that the Kid was still alive and had been living in Texas under an alias, as recently as the previous year. Hines also identified another man, a veteran of the Lincoln County War, who resided in California and who had visited with the Kid only months earlier. Despite insistent questioning by Morrison, Hines never revealed the name of the California man. He also refused to identify the exact location of the Kid and the alias he was using.

After concluding Hines's legal affairs, Morrison retained a keen curiosity about what he had learned from his client. During subsequent searches for information concerning the claim that Billy the Kid was still alive and residing in Texas, Morrison was referred to another oldtimer, one in Missouri who knew the true identity of the man Hines identified as the Kid. Morrison located the old fellow, paid him a visit, and drove away with a slip of paper on which was written the name O. L. Roberts and an address in the small town of Hamilton, Texas. Several days later, Morrison contacted O. L. Roberts by letter and made arrangements to travel to central Texas to meet with him.

On a warm day in June 1948, Morrison arrived in Hamilton, a quiet community of some three thousand residents and the seat of Hamilton County. After checking into a hotel, he drove around and located Roberts's address, a small, run-down frame house in need of painting in an unpretentious part of town.

As Morrison climbed the weathered plank steps to the porch, an elderly man opened the screen door, stepped outside, and introduced himself as Roberts. Morrison recalled that the man was wearing a sleeveless sweat shirt, jeans, and cowboy boots. Morrison was impressed by the apparently excellent physical condition of a man he reasoned to be close to ninety years of age. He later described Roberts as being about five feet, eight inches tall and weighing around 165 pounds. The "smiling, blue-gray eyes" of the old man caught Morrison's attention immediately, as did the strong handshake. Roberts's hands were noticeably small, with well-shaped fingers and unusually large wrists. The forearms and biceps were quite muscular. The hair lying above his high forehead was thinning. One of Roberts's most prominent features was his large ears, the left one extending farther from the head than the right.

After exchanging greetings, Morrison was invited into the house and introduced to Mrs. Roberts. Following a brief exchange of small talk, Morrison commented that he found it difficult to believe he was in the presence of the outlaw Billy the Kid. According to Morrison, Roberts turned red with embarrassment and informed the visitor that he was mistaken. The Kid, he said, was his half brother who was currently living in Mexico.

Confused and disappointed, Morrison remained to visit with Roberts for another hour as Melinda went about her housekeeping chores in an adjacent room. As Morrison spoke, Roberts often glanced around to ascertain whether Melinda was listening. During their conversation, Morrison told Roberts that he would like to go to Mexico to try to find Billy the Kid and interview him. As Morrison rose to leave, Roberts leaned close and whispered to him that he would like to meet with him again the next day, in private.

The following morning, Morrison arrived at Roberts's home just as the old man was sending his wife out on an errand. Once alone with Morrison, Roberts confessed that he was the outlaw Billy the Kid. He also informed Morrison that his real name was William Henry Roberts and that he had lived employing aliases for most of his life. The name Oliver L. Roberts was one such alias, a name he appropriated from a deceased relative and had been using for many years.

Before Morrison could respond, Roberts cautioned him not to disclose his secret to anyone. In fact, he said that his wife was not even aware of his true identity and that she believed the story that the real Billy the Kid was a relative living in Mexico.

Roberts then told Morrison that he was hesitant about providing any more information and that, above all else, he wanted to be pardoned for a crime for which he had been found guilty but did not commit. Roberts explained that he was aware he had done wrong when he was younger, but since fleeing New Mexico in 1881 he had led a useful and honest life. As he spoke, Roberts began to tremble, tears flooding his eyes and flowing down his weathered face. Sobbing, he told Morrison of his life, of running and hiding and living in constant fear of being recognized by long-time enemies and of being arrested or gunned down. Roberts was convinced that Billy the Kid was still under sentence to be hanged for the killing of sheriff William Brady.

When he finished, Roberts wiped the tears from his face, looked up at Morrison, and asked the visitor if there was any way he could help him

clear his name. Morrison, deeply touched, was skeptical. He needed
more evidence that the man who stood before him was Billy the Kid.

At Morrison's request, Roberts removed his shirt and pants, expos-
ing flesh marked and scarred with what were apparently numerous
bullet and knife wounds, more than twenty-five in all. At each question, Roberts identified the source of one scar or another, including
the one from the bullet he took in the hip when he retrieved a gun
from the body of Sheriff Brady during a shootout at Lincoln.

Morrison reminded Roberts of the oft-told story that Billy the Kid
was able to slip through a pair of handcuffs with ease. In response,
Roberts unhesitatingly held out his hands and tucked each thumb in-
side his palms, clearly making his hands narrower than his wrists.
That, he said, was how he slipped the cuffs during his escape from the
Lincoln County Courthouse.

Throughout the rest of the morning the two men conversed, with
Morrison asking questions and with Roberts responding. When
speaking of his murder trial in Mesilla, where he was sentenced to
hang, tears again filled the old man's eyes as he told of how he had
been unfairly treated and of how Governor Lew Wallace broke his
promise of a pardon for the killing of Sheriff Brady.

The two men spoke of other things that day, and as he listened to
Roberts, Morrison became convinced that the man sitting next to him
possessed an impressive amount of circumstantial knowledge of New
Mexico history as it related to the Lincoln County War. Roberts's fa-
miliarity with historical events, those general and esoteric, was not
gleaned from reading and studying, for he was far from being an ed-
ucated man and could barely read and write. His knowledge—detailed, precise, and thorough—could only have come from personal
experience. The man seated before him, Morrison concluded, must
have been there—that much was obvious from his vivid descriptions
of people, places, and events.

As the noon hour approached, Morrison, notebook in hand, rose to
leave. Before departing, however, he made a promise to Roberts: he
told the old man he would discuss his request for a pardon with an acquaintance who headed a law firm. If granted approval, he would
prepare the necessary papers seeking clemency. Morrison further
promised Roberts that, according to his wishes, he would keep his
identity secret until the pardon was obtained.

Morrison also made arrangements with Roberts for the two men to
travel to Lincoln and DeBaca counties, New Mexico. Morrison wanted to
cover the region where Billy the Kid worked, roamed, and fought. He

wanted to ask Roberts pointed questions about the various aspects of the history and geography of the area, and he wanted Roberts to try to recall incidents that might have some bearing on his request for a pardon.

The journey, which began on August 16, 1948, lasted several days. During that time a remarkable story unfolded, a story that would remain controversial for the next several decades. As the two men drove through the New Mexico countryside, the life and times of William Henry Roberts, alias Billy the Kid, began to emerge and take shape.

And an incredible life it was. Even if Roberts were not Billy the Kid, his adventures during his previous eighty-nine years were fascinating and captivating. For the first twenty-one years of Roberts's life, however, there emerged a curious and rather logical blending with what was known and presumed to be known about the life of Billy the Kid. Keen insights into a variety of events and personalities were offered by the old man that cleared up historical confusions or shed light onto previously unknown events. Information was offered that, at the time, was generally unknown to historians, much of which was subsequently verified.

Morrison was convinced that Roberts, if he were not Billy the Kid, must surely have been a close compatriot of the outlaw, for his knowledge of and insight into the outlaw's activities and motivations as well as the region's history, geography, and personalities were extensive and detailed.

After accumulating a massive amount of information on Roberts, including several reels of taped conversations, Morrison brought it to noted Southwestern historian, folklorist, and writer Dr. C. L. Sonnichsen. With Morrison's help, Sonnichsen, a professor at Texas Western College, now the University of Texas at El Paso, authored a book about Roberts titled *Alias Billy the Kid*, which was published in 1955 by the University of New Mexico Press. How ironic, mused Sonnichsen in print, if after "almost seventy years of running and hiding from the law, this man Roberts comes forth, all atear and atremble, with what must be one of the most amazing stories of all time and nobody believed him."

On a cool day in November 1950, William Henry Roberts's story became part of the public record when he, accompanied by Morrison, went before the governor of New Mexico requesting a pardon. Almost immediately, a cry arose from a core of Billy the Kid enthusiasts, from descendants of Pat Garrett, and from others that Roberts was a fake, an imposter, and not to be taken seriously. The detractors insisted Roberts lacked credibility, that he could not be the outlaw Billy the Kid.

FOUR

❖❖❖

William Henry Roberts's Story, Part I: 1859–1881

Derived from tapes, transcriptions of oral accounts, the personal notes of Morrison, the collection of Roberts's stepgrandson, and in part from the book *Alias Billy the Kid* by C. L. Sonnichsen and William V. Morrison, the following are pertinent recollections of William Henry Roberts.

Because of lapses in Roberts's memory, mispronounced words, grammatical errors, as well as mistakes in Morrison's note taking and in Sonnichsen and Frederic Bean's transcribing, corrections have been made to misspellings, grammar, and historical and geographical references for clarity and continuity. These corrections do not compromise Roberts's version of events. Quotations and indented paragraphs represent the actual words of William Henry Roberts transcribed from tape recordings made by Morrison in 1949.

ORIGINS

William Henry Roberts was born near Buffalo Gap in present-day Taylor County, Texas, on December 31, 1859. During this time, Buffalo Gap was only a tiny settlement known to the few homesteaders in the region and to occasional travelers who passed through the area. Many years later it gained the status of a community and could be found on maps.

Roberts's father, James Henry Roberts, was born March 8, 1832, near Lexington, Kentucky. His mother was the former Mary Adeline Dunn, also from Kentucky.

James Henry Roberts, often called "Wild Henry," was a rough and temperamental sort, a former Indian fighter given to violence. When the Civil War broke out, he left his family in Buffalo Gap in the care of neighbors and enlisted in the Confederacy. Not long after the elder

Roberts departed Buffalo Gap, Mary Adeline died, leaving the toddler William Henry, whom they called Billy, temporarily orphaned and living with neighbors.

Weeks later, Mary Adeline's half sister, Katherine Ann Bonney, arrived from Indian Territory and took the youth to raise. Within a few months, Bonney traveled with Billy to Trinidad, Colorado. She left no information regarding her destination because she did not want Wild Henry, whom she considered an unfit father, to follow her and reclaim the child. From Colorado, Bonney and young Billy Roberts traveled to and lived in several locations until finally arriving at Santa Fe, New Mexico. There, she married William Antrim on March 1, 1873. Soon after, the family moved to Silver City. Young Billy Roberts, now thirteen or fourteen years old and believed by everyone to be Katherine's son, went by the name Billy Antrim.

While living in Silver City, Billy became acquainted with another youth, named Jesse Evans. Years later Evans, with Roberts, would become a prominent figure in New Mexico's Lincoln County War.

At the end of the Civil War, Wild Henry Roberts returned to Buffalo Gap to learn of the death of his wife and the disappearance of his son. Repeated inquiries into the location of Billy proved futile. Wild Henry eventually married a young woman named Elizabeth Ferguson. A son, James, was born to the union in 1867.

REUNION

Billy Roberts left New Mexico in late 1872 and returned to Buffalo Gap, where he learned that his father, stepmother, and half brother had moved to Carlton, Texas, some sixty miles to the east-southeast. After locating them, he moved in and remained for almost two years. Billy, still in his early teens, was small for his age and was called "Kid" Roberts by neighbors.

Wild Henry, described as a battle-scarred veteran and a man of little sensitivity, was proficient in riding, roping, and shooting—important frontier skills that he passed to his two sons. By the time he was fifteen years old, Billy "Kid" Roberts was an accomplished horseman and pistol shot, manifesting his shooting skills with both hands.

One day, following a violent disagreement over the breaking of some horses, Billy received a severe whipping at the hands of Wild Henry. As soon as he was able to travel, he packed his few belongings and the Roberts family Bible and left for Indian Territory. There he found a job as a cowhand trailing a small herd of longhorns and working his way up a cattle trail into Oklahoma.

TRAVELS AND OUTLAWS

Billy quit the cattle herd at a place called Briartown, in Oklahoma, and continued northward on foot until he met a rider heading in the same direction. After exchanging greetings, the stranger invited Billy to climb up behind him, and together they rode to a nearby ranch. Here, Billy met a woman named Belle Reed, later to become known as Belle Starr, a famous Oklahoma outlaw. Billy was offered a job as a general chore boy and occasionally served as a lookout. During the time he spent there, he met a number of Belle Reed's acquaintances: Frank and Jesse James, the Younger brothers, and the outlaws Rube and Jim Burrows.

After three months at the outlaw hideout, Billy expressed a desire to leave. Belle, who called the youth the Texas Kid, provided him with a new set of clothes and fifty dollars. After bidding her goodbye, Billy returned to Silver City to visit his aunt, Katherine Antrim.

Not long after Billy's arrival, Katherine died on September 16, 1874. Having no reason to remain in Silver City, he returned to Indian Territory, where he fell in with a gang of cattle rustlers. Billy was little more than a camp lackey for the outlaws, who occasionally beat him. One man, however, stood up for the youth, gave him a gun, and encouraged him to leave.

Weeks later, Billy Roberts arrived in Dodge City, Kansas, where he found work breaking horses. Before long, he was offered a job doing the same thing in South Dakota. For the next two years, Roberts, who was now going by the name Billy Bonney, traveled to Arizona, Montana, Oregon, Wyoming, and Nebraska, all the while earning his living as a bronc buster and cowhand.

In April 1877, Billy arrived in Arizona and found work on a ranch near the Gila River. At the beginning of the summer, he traveled to Mesilla, New Mexico, where he encountered his old friend Jesse Evans. Evans was running with a gang of toughs that included Jimmy McDaniel, Billy Morton, Frank Baker, and Tom O'Keefe.

A short time later, Roberts, also known as Billy Bonney, left Mesilla for Phoenix, New Mexico. A portion of the trip took him through the rugged Guadalupe Mountains on the Texas–New Mexico border, where he encountered some hostile Indians. Following a brief skirmish, he lost his horse and fled the region on foot, eventually winding up at the Jones Ranch near Seven Rivers. Jim and John Jones were working for John Chisum's large ranch near Roswell. There, Billy found employment herding cattle to the railhead at Dodge City.

THE KID COMES TO LINCOLN COUNTY

After working at Chisum's for a few months, Billy Roberts took a job with Pete Maxwell at Bosque Redondo. From there, he went to work on Frank Coe's ranch near the Ruidoso River. While employed by Coe, Billy ran into Jesse Evans and Frank Baker once again.

Evans and Baker were working for a man named Lawrence G. Murphy, and their job was to steal cattle from John Chisum. Murphy was a Lincoln businessman and, with Emil Fritz, held a monopoly that supplied beef to the Mescalero Indian reservation. Roberts fell in with Evans and Baker for a time, but after a disagreement concerning the division of some stolen horses, he left the gang and found a job on the Tunstall Ranch, near the Rio Feliz.

Here, Roberts became acquainted with Tunstall's foreman, Dick Brewer. He also met several men with whom he was to ride during the next few months, including Charlie Bowdre, John Middleton, Doc Skurlock, Bob Widenmann, Tom O'Folliard, Dave Rudabaugh, and others.

After working in the area for several weeks, Roberts grew aware of a growing conflict between Tunstall and Murphy. Tunstall, with his partner McSween, owned and operated a store in the town of Lincoln, which represented competition to one of Murphy's retail enterprises. In addition, Tunstall and McSween wanted some of the government beef contracts held by Murphy. Each faction accused the other of stealing each other's cattle, but the Murphy cartel had the backing of influential politicians, judges, and lawyers, all a loose organization known as the Santa Fe Ring. Lincoln County sheriff William Brady favored the Murphy enterprises and remained hostile to anyone associated with the Tunstall–McSween organization. During a taped interview with Morrison, Roberts recalled that the trouble all started when "lawyer McSween had been hired by the Murphy bunch to prosecute some of the Chisum cowboys for rustling cattle, but when he found out the Chisum boys were only taking back Chisum cows that were stolen by Murphy's men," McSween switched sides and "joined up with Tunstall."

Roberts said the "Murphy–Dolan Ring operated a store where they sold supplies to the ranches, and then John Tunstall came along and opened his own store. That's where the trouble really started, between the two stores. McSween formed a partnership with Tunstall while he worked a case for Emil Fritz."

TUNSTALL'S MURDER

Following the death of Emil Fritz, Murphy went into partnership with James J. Dolan and soon afterward obtained a judgment against McSween for some money that was owed. The courts declared that Murphy was legally entitled to attach certain Tunstall–McSween property. Some cattle had been turned over as partial recompense, and Tunstall decided to drive several head of horses into Lincoln to settle the debt once and for all. On the morning of February 18, 1878, Tunstall climbed aboard his wagon and—accompanied by Billy Roberts, Dick Brewer, Robert Widenmann, and John Middleton— began herding the horses toward Lincoln.

Earlier that day, according to Roberts, Tunstall ordered the four cowhands to round up the horses "so we could take them into town until the case was settled in court." Dolan had assembled a posse made up, in Robert's words, "of a bunch of cutthroats and outlaws . . . to head out to Tunstall's ranch for the herd of horses." Roberts remembered the small party was well up in the mountains when they saw the posse coming, one that included Dolan, Billy Morton, Jesse Evans, Frank Baker, and a few others. Roberts told Morrison, "There was a settlement when Fritz died and the Murphy–Dolan Store claimed that Fritz owed a bill of goods. McSween got the settlement money and the Murphy bunch claimed it, so they rode over to Mesilla and got a court order in the form of a writ that would give them some of the goods in McSween's and Tunstall's store" as well as a "herd of blooded horses out at Tunstall's ranch." Sheriff William Brady was given the papers, "and he served them on McSween, padlocking the store until it was settled."

Roberts, Brewer, Widenmann, and Middleton wanted to flee from the oncoming posse and tried to convince Tunstall to join them, but the rancher didn't want to leave the herd untended. Tunstall was also convinced he would not be harmed. As the posse neared, Roberts and his companions "rode off a safe distance to watch, leaving Tunstall with the horses." Roberts said he could tell by the way "that posse came galloping up on us that there was going to be trouble. Roberts and his companions remained on their horses several dozen yards away and partially hidden in some brush watching when Dolan and the posse rode up on Tunstall. They formed a circle around him, and, according to Roberts, "they shot [him] cold blood." He said, "We took off when the shooting started, outnumbered like we were. The posse drove the horses to Lincoln. Later on, the boys went out and got John's body."

Roberts admired Tunstall and believed him to be a decent and honest man, a man who always treated him fairly. When the slain rancher and businessman was laid to rest, the youth swore revenge on those responsible for his murder. "None of the Murphy boys were present at the funeral of John Tunstall when we buried him behind his store. It was a good thing for them that they stayed away. Tunstall was a good man. He was good to me, and he treated me like a gentleman. I lost the best friend I ever had the day they killed him. I swore that day at the funeral that I would make them pay for their dirty deed."

THE REGULATORS

A few days later, justice of the peace John B. Wilson appointed Dick Brewer as constable and provided him with a warrant for the arrest of Tunstall's killers. Brewer enlisted the aid of Roberts (now referring to himself William Antrim) with Henry Brown, Fred Waite, Charlie Bowdre, Frank McNab, and a few others. They called themselves the Regulators and set out to arrest those responsible. Roberts had grown fond of Brewer and was eager to follow his direction. Roberts recalled that Dick Brewer was foreman at the Tunstall Ranch, "so it was up to him what we would do about the way they shot John." According to Roberts, "Brewer told the group that he knew a judge who might be willing to help them." Roberts then suggested that they "ride over and tell him that we were witnesses to the shooting . . . and swear an oath that John never went for a gun. They shot him in cold blood, and we can testify to it."

Judge Wilson, who was a friend to Tunstall and his ranch hands, swore in Dick Brewer as constable and gave him a warrant for the arrest of the slayers. Roberts said, "Dick took me, Henry Brown, Fred Waite, Charlie Bowdre, Frank McNab, and a few others to go after them."

The hunt began for the murderers, who had left Lincoln for their hideout in Seven Rivers country.

Roberts recalled riding up on several of their quarry near the Seven Rivers country. "The shooting started, and most of them got away. But we captured Billy Morton, the leader of the bunch, and Baker, who I'd known at Murphy's cow camp a few months earlier." The two men had once been friends of Billy the Kid, but Roberts said, "I should have killed those boys the day I left."

The Regulators ordered Morton and Baker to mount up for the return ride to the Chisum Ranch, where they would stay overnight before returning to Lincoln, but the two captives never completed the trip. During the following morning, the group stopped at Roswell. Roberts remembered, "We suspected that Murphy's boys would be waiting for us on the road to Lincoln, so we went on the north road, over the mountains. We stopped at Agua Negra in the Capitans, where an argument started" between McCloskey and one of the posse members, Frank McNab. McNab killed McCloskey during the argument. "Then Morton and Baker both tried to make a run for it. I didn't want to take any chance of losing them, so I had to shoot them. We went on to Lincoln that day without our prisoners."

In the meantime, Sheriff Brady had been issued warrants for the arrest of Billy Bonney for cattle theft. Brady caught up with him at Seven Rivers, placed him under arrest, and took possession of his pistol—a pearl-handled .44 caliber. When Roberts was later released on bond, Brady kept the pistol.

On the morning of April 1, Sheriff Brady, Deputy Hindman, county clerk Billy Mathews, John Long, and George Peppin were walking down the main street of Lincoln toward the courthouse when they were spotted by Roberts. The Kid, with Brown, Middleton, Waite, and two black men, hid behind an adobe wall near the Tunstall store. As Brady and his companions passed near the wall, the Regulators opened fire. Roberts aimed at Mathews but missed. Brady was killed instantly, and Hindman, severely wounded, died a short time later. Mathews, Long, and Peppin scattered and took cover.

Despite the passage of so many years, Roberts recalled the event clearly. He related that he and Hindman "had a run-in a few days before, but my bullet missed him." On this morning, Roberts aimed at Mathews but missed him again. "The other boys were firing at the same time. Brady fell dead on the spot. Hindman died soon after, but Mathews got away and ran behind an adobe wall down the street."

When the smoke cleared, Roberts and Fred Waite leapt over the wall and ran to where Brady lay in the street. Roberts retrieved his pearl-handled .44 from Brady's body, "the one he'd taken from me when he arrested me on cattle-rustling warrants. I'd paid twenty-five dollars for that pearl-handled Colt down in San Antone and I thought a lot of that gun."

Just as Roberts was removing his pistol from Brady's holster, "Mathews fired a rifle from behind the wall where he was hiding. The bullet caught me high on my right hip, tearing the flesh when it went through me. Then, it clipped Waite through the leg. We got back over the wall; then we found our horses and rode hard away from Lincoln. I wasn't hurt much, but Waite was laid up for a few days. Brady and his men were armed with rifles and six-shooters. They would have killed us if they had gotten the chance."

Three days later, April 4, while the Regulators were hiding out at Blazer's Mill in the wake of the Brady killing, Andrew "Buckshot" Roberts arrived. Buckshot, believed to be a member of the posse that killed Tunstall, was unaware of the presence of the Regulators at the mill.

Roberts claimed that "old Buckshot Roberts, he was worse than any of them. He was out to get our scalps for the lousy money on our heads. He never fought in the cattle war. He was an outlaw before he came to that country. I know that for a fact. He was a snake, too. But he got what was coming to him that day at Blazer's place."

Roberts told Morrison that Buckshot had been run out of Texas by the Rangers and landed in Lincoln County. While riding with Murphy's cowhands, Buckshot came to San Patricio, where Roberts was living, with the intention of chasing the young outlaw out of the country. A few days before riding up to Blazer's Mill, Buckshot found Charlie Bowdre and started an argument with him. Roberts recalled, "I came out unexpectedly and ran him off with my six-shooter, but he came back that night as Charlie and I were leaving. He shot at us, but we rode out of it. That's the reason I was trying so hard to kill him at Blazer's."

Roberts explained that the Regulators had warrants for Buckshot's arrest. "Dick was a deputy, and me and Bowdre were with him. We shot it out with Buckshot and he [killed] Brewer. He almost got me one time, but Bowdre finally got Buckshot and that was the end of it."

Following the shootout at Blazer's Mill, "We went into hiding. John Coughlan was appointed sheriff of Lincoln County and succeeded Brady; then Dad Peppin was made the sheriff. Before he was appointed, Dad Peppin worked for Coughlan, who was buying and selling our cattle. We would take a herd of horses up to Tascosa to sell, and we drove cattle back for Coughlan at Three Rivers. Peppin skimmed stolen cattle, too; he did. That was rough country back then."

THE LINCOLN COUNTY WAR

Events in Lincoln County were about to come to a close. In fear for his life, McSween had taken refuge at the Chisum Ranch but was escorted back to Lincoln by the Regulators. As the group rode into town, sheriff George Peppin, who replaced Brady and who was now accompanied by several deputies, began shooting at them. "They had started firing on us when we rode in that day," remembered Roberts, "so we fought them back."

Fleeing from the attack, the Regulators sought refuge in the McSween home and the nearby Tunstall store. Peppin's men and other Murphy–Dolan supporters sought for and found suitable firing positions in the Murphy–Dolan store and on the hillside facing McSween's house.

For the next four days, occasional gunshots were exchanged, but little harm was done. On July 19, Colonel N. A. M. Dudley, leading a company of black troopers, rode into Lincoln from Fort Stanton and ordered McSween to cease firing but said nothing to the opposing force.

Roberts related that McSween told Dudley, "They started it. As long as they shoot at us, we intend to protect ourselves." Roberts recalled that Dudley told McSween that "he wouldn't interfere, that the sheriff had the matter in hand, but then he cornered some of our men and ran them off."

Later that afternoon, someone set fire to the McSween house, and as it burned, the black soldiers stationed on the hillside began shooting. Roberts insisted, "We had them whipped until the army came into town. If we could have kept the soldiers out there at Stanton, we would have whipped Peppin's posse. We didn't lose any men until that night, and we'd gotten a few of their men up on that hillside."

As Roberts recalled the events of that day, he grew agitated at the intrusion of Colonel Dudley and his soldiers, knowing they had been invited to the fray by Murphy and had turned it into a one-sided shooting match. "While the house was burning," recalled Roberts, "Mrs. McSween entered Dudley's camp and begged him to stop the fighting. He said he didn't have the authority to interfere, but some of his soldiers were up on that hill firing at us with the Murphy men."

Around dusk, with the house almost completely burned down except for the kitchen, the Regulators decided to make a break for the river. Roberts remembered that "the door opened on the northwest corner into an area between the house and an adobe wall. There was a board fence between the house and the corral, running north and south, with a gate at the northeast corner of the yard. Tunstall's store building was east of the board fence on the other side of the corral where he kept the horses. Some of the Murphy men were just across the river, which ran past the north of the house. The gate in the board fence opened toward Tunstall's store."

Roberts said that someone opened the back door and looked out just as Bob Beckwith and some soldiers tried to rush the house. Harvey Morris, who was studying law with McSween, led the way out of the kitchen door. He was followed by Roberts, Jose Chavez, McSween, Vicente Romero, and Francisco Zamora. Morris was shot down immediately just in front of Roberts. As Roberts came through the door, he spotted Bob Beckwith and shot him, convinced that "one of my bullets killed him when I made a run for it."

Roberts "ran through the gate with both .44s blazing and Jose Chavez was right behind me. He and I ran toward Tunstall's store. We got fired at, and then we turned toward the river where . . . there was brush and undergrowth to hide us."

Roberts said that a bullet went through his hat as he ran through the gate. Firing their pistols, he and Chavez ran toward the nearby Rio Penasco river bottom in search of cover. As they crossed the river, Roberts lost his hat and one revolver.

McSween, Romero, and Zamora made it to the gate but, according to Roberts, were forced back to a small enclosure between the burning building and the adobe wall by heavy gunfire from Murphy's men and the soldiers. They made a second attempt but were all gunned down, as Roberts learned later, "by Jones and McKinney and those soldiers of Dudley's." O'Folliard, Yginio Salazar, and several others made a dash for freedom seconds later. All escaped save for Salazar, who was struck by a bullet and fell near the door. The soldiers and deputies left the Mexican for dead, but when the commotion died down, the wounded Salazar crawled away under cover of night.

Referring to Salazar, Roberts said, "They thought he was dead, but he crawled out that night after everyone left. He told me how McSween and the rest got killed." After escaping from the Tunstall house, Roberts and some of the Regulators fled to San Patricio, where they hid out for several days. "I met Tom O'Folliard at Gallego's house in San Patricio a few days afterward," Roberts recalled. "Tom saw all of it—he was still in the burning house when McSween and the others got shot."

Roberts said, "We didn't know it then, but that fight we lost at McSween's was the turning point for us in the war. With McSween and Tunstall dead, we didn't have a way to make a living. We drifted down to San Patricio for a while, but there were warrants out for us and we had to stay on the dodge. I was bitter about what they'd done to McSween and Tunstall. I rustled some cattle from the Murphy herds when I could find them so we could eat and make a living the only way that was left for us. I had wanted to settle down and live in that country, but they wouldn't let me. They made outlaws of us. We had to make a living some way."

For the next few months, while ranging from Fort Sumner to Portales, Roberts and his companions earned their living by rounding up stray cattle in the area and selling them to anyone who would buy them. During this time, Roberts was blamed for the killing of Indian agent Morris Bernstein, a killing he denied.

ENTER WALLACE

In the winter of 1879, Roberts met with James Dolan and Jesse Evans in Lincoln, and all agreed to stop warring with one another. Roberts recalled, "Tom O'Folliard and I got together with J. J. Dolan and Jesse Evans to talk about things. A fellow named Campbell was along with Dolan and Evans. The five of us talked about all the trouble we'd had in the past, and we agreed to stop fighting each other. I thought Dolan and Evans were on the level about ending the trouble we had. Now that Tunstall and McSween were dead, Tom and I didn't have much of a stake in things. Tom and I shook hands with Dolan and Evans, agreeing that the fight was over. When we walked out of that saloon, we parted company."

As they were leaving the saloon after the meeting, they encountered Huston I. Chapman, a lawyer for Mrs. McSween. From a short distance away, Roberts and O'Folliard watched as Chapman walked up to Dolan, Evans, and Campbell. "Words were said," Roberts recalled, "and then Dolan and Campbell pulled their six-shooters, shot Chapman in cold blood. Me and Tom were standing right there, and we saw the whole thing. With the warrants that were out on me, I couldn't afford to take a hand in it, so I told Tom we ought to clear out of there as quick as we could."

Early in 1879, Roberts learned that Governor Lew Wallace issued an offer to him of one thousand dollars if he would turn himself in and testify against the illegal activities of the Dolan faction.

We holed up in San Patricio, laying low, wondering what would come of the shooting. One day a fellow brought word that Governor Wallace had offered a thousand dollars if I would come in and give myself up for the murder of Chapman. I had it figured for a trap right at first.

Word around the territory was that Governor Wallace was doing his best to clean up the mess around Lincoln, and he was looking into the cattle contracts controlled by the Catron ring up in Santa Fe. Catron was behind the Murphy–Dolan bunch. It looked like the new governor was trying to put a stop to all their crooked dealings.

With this opportunity, Roberts could see a way out of his difficulties. He discussed the issue with friend Tom O'Folliard, suggesting that a meeting with the governor could be arranged to see if he was "on the level." O'Folliard didn't like the idea, but Roberts reminded him "how bad things were for us, how they were forced to hide out and steal cattle and horses to get by." In time, Roberts and O'Folliard agreed to meet with Wallace about the murder of Chapman.

Roberts "had a friend who spelled it out in a letter for me, what I wanted from Governor Wallace," which was amnesty for past crimes. Roberts remembered he was "edgy" about meeting with the governor. He was wanted for rustling cattle. "Me and a few of the boys had been taking cattle from Chisum as pay for the money he promised us," he related. "Old John thought he could get off without paying us for what we did in the war, now that McSween was dead. We cut cattle out of Chisum's herd, and he didn't do anything about it. He knew he owed us, he did. They made outlaws of us, so I was edgy about meeting with the governor. They had fresh warrants out on us for rounding up those cattle."

Wallace wrote back and agreed to meet the Kid at the home of John B. Wilson in Lincoln. Wallace and Billy met in March and spoke for several hours. Roberts described how he and Tom O'Folliard had seen Dolan shoot down lawyer Chapman.

I rode in with Tom and tied my horse while Tom kept watch outside. I went in through the back door. The governor and Wilson were alone in the house. We talked for several hours. I explained that Tom and I had seen Campbell and Dolan shoot Chapman in a cold-blooded murder that night. The governor wanted me and Tom to testify before the grand jury and tell them what we saw. He also wanted me to testify against Colonel Dudley in his court martial at Stanton. I told him about things in general in this country and what started the trouble. I was not afraid to talk like the rest of them were. I had the guts to help the governor out. No one else would say enough to help him.

Before leaving, Wallace promised to pardon him if Roberts would agree to stand trial for the killing of Sheriff Brady. The governor even promised to have his personal lawyer, Ira E. Leonard, represent the young outlaw. In turn, Roberts promised to cooperate if all parties agreed that he was to stand trial only in Lincoln. Wallace assured him this would be the case, and left.

I had that talk with the governor one night in March. We didn't meet like they say we did—in the daytime at Patron's. I had only this one meeting with Governor Wallace until I was arrested. The governor promised to pardon me if I would stand trial on my indictments in Lincoln. I also agreed to testify against Dudley at his court martial hearing at Fort Stanton and testify before the grand jury in the Chapman case. I promised to do it, and we shook hands on it before Tom and I left Squire Wilson's that night. The governor promised that he would send Sheriff Kimball down to San Patricio to arrest me, and [he] allowed me to pick the men who would come with Kimball so none of them would be my enemies. Governor Wallace gave me his promise that he would appoint Judge Leonard, his personal lawyer, to defend me. I had the word of the governor on all these things before I left Squire Wilson's house.

Billy, with O'Folliard, returned to San Patricio. Several days later, sheriff George Kimball, who replaced Peppin, came to San Patricio with the men the Kid asked for, arrested him and O'Folliard, and re-turned them to the jail at Lincoln.

When Billy's case was called before the court, Leonard was nowhere to be seen. Instead, the court appointed Colonel Albert J. Fountain to represent him. Billy pleaded not guilty to the indictments and gave testimony against Dolan and his men for the killing of Chapman. Shortly after, he was taken to Fort Stanton to testify at the Dudley court martial. Following that, the judge ordered the Kid transported to Mesilla to stand trial. The agreement with Governor Wallace that the Kid would be tried only in Lincoln was not to be fulfilled, and by this time the governor had distanced himself from the process. Roberts recalled, "The judge over in Mesilla was Warren Bristol, and he was a Murphy sympathizer and a friend of Tom Catron at the head of the Santa Fe ring. I knew I couldn't get a fair trial at Mesilla under Judge Bristol. The governor hadn't kept his promise to me. Something had gone wrong."

Disturbed by Wallace's broken promises and concerned he would not receive a fair trial, Roberts, with O'Folliard, escaped from the Lincoln jail and returned to Fort Sumner. For the next several months, he and his companions resumed their cattle-rustling activities to make a living.

Roberts told Morrison, "They never arrested anyone else for the Brady shooting. They pinned the whole affair on me because they wanted to get rid of Billy the Kid. The governor broke his word to me. I did what I promised I would do, but he didn't keep his promise to me."

To make a living, Roberts went back to stealing cattle and horses. "We were wanted by the law, and they put out new warrants for us. We had to make a living, and rustling cattle was about all that was left for us, being wanted men. We got word that they were organizing a posse to come after us and that the Murphy bunch had picked Carlyle to head up the posse and hunt us down."

On December 1, 1880, the Kid and several of his companions were staying at the Greathouse Ranch near White Oaks. While there, the posse that was searching for Billy the Kid, Billy Wilson, and Dave Rudabaugh surrounded the ranch house and called for the outlaws to give themselves up. Presently, James Carlyle, a White Oaks resident and deputy, was sent in personally to demand a surrender, but he presented no warrant. Roberts said that Carlyle "came to the house to try to talk us into giving ourselves up without a fight." Roberts asked Carlyle for a warrant, and the deputy told him he didn't need one, that "everybody in the territory knows you're a wanted man for killing Sheriff Brady. I wear a badge, and that's good enough to bring you in. This badge is all I need."

The outlaws decided to hold Carlyle hostage until an escape could be effected. In turn, rancher Greathouse was captured by the posse, who made it known that unless Carlyle was released, Greathouse would be shot. According to Roberts, "Just then someone outside fired a shot. Carlyle whirled around, figuring one of my boys had started a move to fight our way out of the house. Carlyle dove for the front window. When he broke through the glass, his own men started firing, figuring it was me trying to make a break for it. They shot him, and he fell dead on the porch. Not one of my men had fired a shot—Carlyle's own posse killed him. When the posse saw Carlyle was dead, they pulled out. We waited until it got dark and we slipped away from the ranch."

The following day, the posse returned and burned down the ranch house, thinking the Regulators were still inside, but they had fled to Las Vegas during the night. At Las Vegas, Roberts learned that he was being blamed for the killing of Carlyle. At that point, he dictated another letter to Governor Wallace explaining he was innocent of any wrongdoing in the death of the deputy.

ENTER GARRETT

Leading the search for Billy the Kid was sheriff Pat Garrett, a former buffalo hunter and cowhand. Garrett once worked for Pete Maxwell but didn't remain long. He had been a deputy under George Kimball, but when election time came he, backed by John Chisum and others, ran and won.

Roberts had known Garrett earlier in Texas, and when the lanky lawman arrived in Lincoln County nearly penniless, the Kid, with a few friends, pooled their money and bought him a new pair of boots and paid for his wedding reception.

Garrett had been a deputy under Kimball. When Kimball ran for reelection, John Chisum, Lea, and several others put Garrett up to run against him. Those men knew that Kimball was a friend of the governor and a friend of Billy the Kid. Garrett won the election, but he had a lot of help from powerful men who wanted Kimball out of office.

Garrett had not been in that country long. He had come over from Texas after he had shot his partner in an argument over some buffalo hides. Garrett was nothing when he landed in Fort Sumner. Me and some of the boys bought him the first pair of boots he ever owned when he got there, and we took up a collection to pay for the celebration at his first wedding in Fort Sumner. He rode with us some . . . gambled and danced and was just one of the boys back then. He went to work for Maxwell right at first, but he didn't last long. Then he went in with Beaver Smith, who owned a lunchroom and saloon. Folks didn't have much use for Garrett at that time.

Garrett, eager to improve his position in the community and advance his political career, was anxious to capture the most wanted man in the region, Billy the Kid. Roberts insisted that "with the killing of Carlyle tacked on me, Garrett now had an excuse to come after me."

One evening Garrett and his deputies hid in the home of Charlie Bowdre, near Fort Sumner, and waited for the Regulators to arrive. As they rode in, Roberts grew suspicious and, leaving the group, took another route to the house. "We were riding in a snowstorm in December, heading to Fort Sumner. It was about eight o'clock at night, and we headed for Bowdre's house, where O'Folliard had been staying with Bowdre and his wife. As we rode in, I scouted around to see if anybody was around town watching for us. The rest of the boys rode straight in. Garrett and his posse were waiting for us. They had taken over Bowdre's house, setting a trap for me. Tom and the others rode right up to the house and the shooting started."

O'Folliard, mortally wounded, was knocked from his horse. After the Regulators fled, O'Folliard was carried into the house, where he died. Tip McKinney, a member of Garrett's posse, was O'Folliard's cousin, but when the dying outlaw begged for water, the deputy refused to give him any.

Roberts felt guilty about his friend's death. Earlier that year in Roswell, he met O'Folliard's uncle, a man named Cook, who wanted his nephew to leave the outlaws and come home. The Kid, however, insisted that O'Folliard remain, telling him he was badly needed.

Several days later, on December 23, with snow on the ground, the Regulators arrived at an old rock house at Stinking Springs. Deciding to spend the night in the abandoned structure, they led two of the horses inside to help protect them from the cold. Roberts remembered the incident well. "Early the next morning, Charlie Bowdre went out to feed the horses. When he stepped through the opening where the front door had been, Garrett and his posse fired from ambush without any warning. Charlie wore a big hat like mine. I figure they thought Charlie was me since it was early and the light was bad. Bowdre took a bullet and called out to us. He ran back through the opening and fell dead right there at my feet, with bullets flying all around that were meant for me. We stayed holed up in that house all day, planning to make a break for it after dark."

When some of the Regulators tried to lead their horses into the rock house, one of the animals was shot and fell dead in the middle of the doorway. The Kid mounted his own horse in an attempt to escape, but he couldn't get it to jump over the dead one. Finally, the group surrendered. "They promised to protect us if we surrendered peacefully," Roberts said. "With the dead horse blocking our way, there was no other way out of the old house. With Bowdre and O'Folliard weighing heavily on my mind, we tossed out our guns and gave ourselves up to Garrett and his posse."

According to Roberts, as the outlaws filed out the door of the rock house, "I saw Tip McKinney, Tom's cousin, and I asked him how it went for Tom. He told me Tom was dead, and he sounded like he was proud of it." The posse loaded the outlaws in a wagon with Bowdre's body and hauled them to Fort Sumner. The next day, Bowdre was interred next to Tom O'Folliard in the Fort Sumner cemetery.

At Fort Sumner, while Billy was chained to Dave Rudabaugh, Pete Maxwell's wife sent her Indian servant girl to ask Garrett if the Kid could visit with the family for awhile. Deputy Jim East escorted the two shackled prisoners to the Maxwell house, where the Indian girl presented Bonney with a scarf she was wearing, one she had recently made from angora. In return, the outlaw gave her a tintype of himself he carried in his shirt pocket. Roberts said, "Mrs. Maxwell asked them to unchain me from Rudabaugh so I could go in the other room to be with the Indian girl. They refused to do it. They suspected it was a trick to let me escape, and they knew about the trick I could pull with the handcuffs."

Two days later, Roberts, now chained to Billy Wilson as well as Rudabaugh, arrived in Las Vegas. The following day, the three were placed aboard a train and taken to Santa Fe. At the capitol, Roberts dictated three letters, which were sent to Governor Wallace reminding him of his earlier promise of amnesty; however, Roberts received no response. During the last week of March, Roberts was taken by stage to Mesilla to stand trial.

The day after they arrived in Las Vegas, "Garrett tried to put us on a train to Santa Fe, but a big crowd showed up at the train station. Garrett thought the mob had come to help me escape, but the crowd wanted Dave Rudabaugh. Rudabuagh had killed a jailer not long before when he escaped from the Las Vegas jail, and the crowd was made up of the dead jailer's friends. I told Garrett that if he would give me a six-shooter, I would help him fight off the mob and I wouldn't give him any trouble about giving it back to him once we got on the train."

THE TRIAL

When Billy the Kid was escorted into the courtroom each morning, he was guarded by Robert Olinger, a U. S. deputy marshall. Olinger was regarded by most who knew him as a bully, and he constantly tormented the Kid. Months earlier, Olinger killed Billy's good friend John Jones by shooting him in the back. Roberts said that Olinger "taunted and threatened me constantly. I tried for a six-shooter on one of my guards one day, but I couldn't quite reach it. I'd have killed Olinger if I had gotten to that gun."

The presiding judge was Warren Bristol, a Murphy–Dolan supporter and a man Billy the Kid once threatened to kill. Roberts said, "Fountain was appointed to represent me on the territorial charge. He did all he could for me. I had no money. They didn't sell my mare up at Scott Moore's in Las Vegas like they said they would. He was a friend of mine, but he claimed I owed him money for boarding the mare."

Though lawyer Fountain did his best to represent the Kid, several important witnesses were never called, and Roberts was convinced that the entire trial was dishonest and rigged from the start. He said, "It was a crooked trial. I asked for witnesses that they said they couldn't find. They didn't want to find them. Sheriff Garrett knew where they were."

As the trial progressed, it dawned on Roberts that he had been set up. None of the other participants in the shooting of Brady and Hindman was arrested.

> Old Dad Peppin testified at my trial . . . that I had killed Sheriff Brady. How did he know who killed anybody? He was the other fellow running down the street with Hindman and Mathews that day Brady was killed. I was trying to shoot Mathews first. Even Pat Garrett admitted to Miguel Otero that he doubted I ever fired a shot at Brady because it was more likely I would have tried to get Mathews since I hated him. Nobody knows who killed Brady and Hindman. There was four against four. Nobody ever tried to find out who killed them either. They blamed Brady's killing on me because of my reputation.

Shackled, handcuffed, and chained to the wooden seat of an army ambulance, the Kid—escorted by Mathews, Olinger, John Kinney, Dave Woods, and two other guards—was transported to Fort Stanton. There, he was picked up by Garrett and taken to the jail at Lincoln. "We left Mesilla a little before midnight so no one would know we were leaving. It took about five days to reach Fort Stanton. As we were sleeping one night, I almost got away from Mathews, who was guarding me at the time. Olinger stuck his gun in my face and told me he wished I would try again, but I didn't."

JAILED

On April 6, Billy the Kid, handcuffed and shackled in leg irons, was chained to the second floor of the Lincoln County Courthouse, formerly the Murphy–Dolan Store. Robert Olinger, assigned to guard the outlaw, continued to threaten and taunt him. One morning, as the deputy loaded his shotgun with buckshot in front of the prisoner, he told Roberts that if he dared attempt escape, he would be shot in the back, with both barrels. The Kid, smiling back at Olinger, told the deputy he might get him first.

Around noon, Olinger, after leaning his shotgun against a wall, uttered several more threats to the young outlaw and then left to escort some prisoners across the street to the Wortley Hotel for lunch. Deputy J. W. Bell was left alone on the second floor to guard the Kid. Unlike Olinger, Bell treated Roberts well, and the two often played cards together.

ESCAPE

After making certain Olinger was inside the hotel, Roberts asked Bell to unlock him so he could go to the privy. Retrieving the key from Garrett's office, Bell opened the lock that held the leg shackles to the floor. Roberts slipped his right hand through the handcuff and slapped the heavy manacle up against Bell's head several times, knocking him to the floor. Roberts immediately grabbed Bell's holstered pistol and ordered the deputy into the armory, where he intended to lock him up while he made his escape. On the way, however, the frightened Bell bolted down the hall toward the stairway. Roberts, legs still contained by the shackles, pursued Bell by jumping and sliding across the wooden floor. As Bell was running down the stairs, Roberts reached the top and fired a shot at the fleeing deputy. The bullet struck the wall and ricocheted into Bell's armpit, passing clean through his body. Bell staggered out the door and died.

Shuffling back up the hall, Roberts retrieved Olinger's double-barreled shotgun. Looking out the open northeast window, he spied the deputy and another man running across the street from the hotel toward the courthouse. As Olinger approached the corner of the building, the Kid pointed the shotgun down at him and said, "Look up, Bob. I want to shoot you in the face with your own buckshot. I don't want to shoot you in the back like you did other men and the Jones boy." With that, Roberts fired, blowing a large hole in the deputy's chest. After Olinger fell, the Kid emptied the second barrel into the lifeless body.

Roberts then ran down the stairs, where he encountered Godfrey Gauss and another man staring at the dead Bell. He told Gauss, who had once been a cook for Tunstall, to cut the chain shackling his legs. At first, Gauss used a saw to try to cut through a link but found it difficult and slow. Finally, he obtained an axe, and with the Kid holding Bell's pistol on him, laid the chain over a rock and chopped the link in half.

While Roberts tied the loose ends of the chain to his belt, a young Mexican named Severo Gallegos saddled a horse that Gauss retrieved from the pasture behind the courthouse. As they brought the horse around to the front of the building, Roberts raced back upstairs to the armory, took two single-action Colt's revolvers and a belt filled with .44-caliber shells, and then returned to the front of the courthouse where the horse was tied.

Encumbered by manacles and weaponry, Roberts climbed on the horse, only to fall off on the opposite side. With the help of the Gallegos youth, he remounted and rode west out of Lincoln to the home of his friend Yginio Salazar, who removed the leg irons.

Salazar tried to convince the Kid that he needed to flee to Mexico to escape the wrath and vengeance of the law, but Roberts replied that he would not leave until he had killed Chisum, Garrett, and Barney Mason. Borrowing a blanket from friend Salazar, Roberts—his revolvers loaded and ready—slept in the brush some distance from the house.

The next day, Roberts borrowed a horse from Salazar and rode toward Fort Sumner. On the way, the horse broke loose and he was left afoot. He walked to Anaya's sheep camp near Fort Sumner and remained for a few days. Traveling by night and sleeping by day, Roberts eventually arrived at the home of Bowdre's widow, where he remained for two days. For the next two-and-a-half months, he worked for and stayed with area ranchers and herders.

Around the middle of May 1881, Roberts rode to Chisum's South Spring Ranch to collect some money, only to discover that the cattleman was gone. He then tried to locate Barney Mason, Garrett's brother-in-law. Mason, unaware of the Kid's presence in the area, nearly rode into his camp. Apparently recognizing the Kid at the last minute, he turned and galloped away.

Roberts had a note sent to Garrett stating that he was looking for him and, after leaving Chisum's ranch, rode back to Fort Sumner and visited with Celsa Gutierrez. Though Celsa was married to Saval Gutierrez, another Garrett brother-in-law, the two spoke of running away to Mexico. Roberts, however, said he wanted to kill Garrett first. While hanging around Fort Sumner, Roberts alternately stayed with Celsa Gutierrez, Jesus Silva, Bowdre's widow, and a rancher named Yerby.

SHOOTING IN FORT SUMNER

Garrett and his deputies, Thomas McKinney and John Poe, soon learned the Kid was in Fort Sumner, and on the evening of July 14 they rode in. During the day, Roberts had been visiting with Garrett's brother-in-law, Saval Gutierrez. Though related by marriage, the Mexican cared little for Garrett. After leaving Saval, Roberts and Celsa went to a dance, accompanied by a friend named Billy Barlow and another woman.

Barlow, believed to be using an alias, had worked with the Kid months earlier on a ranch in Muleshoe, Texas, and had arrived in Lincoln in the winter of 1880. Barlow was slightly younger than the Kid and was of the same size and general appearance.

Following the dance, Roberts, Barlow, and the two women returned to town and stopped at the home of Jesus Silva. Silva informed them that Garrett was in town and was looking for Billy the Kid. About thirty minutes before midnight, the two women left. As he visited with Roberts and Barlow, Silva grew anxious and warned the Kid to leave before Garrett found him. Roberts, unconcerned, told Silva he was hungry, so the Mexican agreed to prepare a meal for him and his friend Barlow.

As Silva busied himself in his kitchen, he informed his two guests that he was out of fresh meat and mentioned that a side of beef was hanging near Maxwell's bedroom. Barlow wanted meat; so, shirtless and in his stockinged feet, he volunteered to go get some.

Minutes after Barlow left the house, the Kid and Silva heard pistol shots. Already on edge as a result of the presence of Garrett, Roberts ran from Silva's room into Maxwell's backyard and began firing his pistols at shadows near the house.

Roberts, easily seen in the moonlit yard, drew return fire from the lawmen. Their first shot struck the Kid in the lower jaw, taking out a tooth as it passed completely through. When he tried to retreat over the fence, a second bullet struck him in the back near the left shoulder.

Once over the fence, Roberts rose and fired back at the shooters, only to be creased by a third bullet, which skimmed across the top of his head, rendering him senseless. Delirious from the concussion and pain, he stumbled into the gallery of a nearby adobe house and, recognized by the lone Mexican woman residing there, was pulled inside. When he regained consciousness some time later, she was holding a piece of beef fat on his head wound to staunch the flow of blood.

While lying on the cot, Roberts asked the woman to reload his pistols for him, which she did. After his head cleared, he was prepared to go back out after Garrett when an excited Celsa Gutierrez entered the house and informed him that the sheriff and his men killed Billy Barlow and were passing the body off as Billy the Kid's. Tearfully, she begged Roberts to flee from the area as quickly as possible.

At 3 A.M. on the morning of July 15, Celsa brought the Kid's horse around to the small adobe where he remained in hiding. A moment later, they were joined by Frank Lobato, a friend of Roberts. After bidding Celsa goodbye, Billy the Kid and Lobato rode away in the darkness.

FIVE

✦✦✦

William Henry Roberts's Story, Part II: 1881–1950

While recounting his past about fleeing Fort Sumner in the wake of Sheriff Garrett's killing of Billy Barlow, William Henry Roberts experienced some difficulty remembering certain events, and he occasionally became confused about dates. He told his interviewer, William Morrison, that sixty-nine years was "a long time to recollect." Roberts's memory, however, was keen when he was recalling circumstances where his life was placed in danger. The following—taken from notes in the possession of Roberts's stepgrandson Bill Allison, quotes and paraphrasings from tapes and transcriptions made by Morrison and Bean, and entries in the Sonnichsen book *Alias Billy the Kid*—traces portions of Roberts's life from the time he left Fort Sumner in 1881 through his death in Hico, Texas. During this time, Roberts used a number of different aliases.

After riding out of Fort Sumner in the early morning of July 15, 1881, Roberts and Frank Lobato stayed at one sheep camp after another until the outlaw's wounds healed enough to permit extended travel. In early August, the Kid went to El Paso and remained with friends for a time. From there, he traveled to the state of Sonora, Mexico, where he lived in a Yaqui Indian village for about two years.

Leaving Mexico, Roberts journeyed to Grand Saline, Texas, a small town about sixty miles east of Dallas. He arrived dressed in the manner of the Yaqui Indians with whom he had lived and soon found a job driving a salt wagon to Carlton, the town where he had last seen his father. Though he made two trips to Carlton, Roberts was unable to locate any relatives.

Months later, Roberts returned to Sonora, where he remained until the arrival of the winter season. At the first snow he ventured back to Texas and was now referring to himself as the Texas Kid. He soon found work with the Powers Cattle Company and a short time later left for Decatur, located about one hundred miles northeast of Carlton. There, he encountered a cowhand he once met while traveling in the Southwest during the early 1870s.

Roberts and his friend signed on with a cattle drive that took them to Kansas City. While there, Roberts was arrested when someone recognized him as Billy the Kid. Though detained for a few days, he was eventually released.

A short time later, Roberts and his friend returned to Decatur and went to work breaking horses for a man named W. T. Waggoner of the famous Waggoner ranching empire. During the winter of 1884, the two friends traveled to the Black Hills of South Dakota, where they worked for three or four years as scouts and guards for a stage line. During this period, Roberts picked up a nickname, Brushy Bill, from riding in the brushy hills of the region. During one of his scouting expeditions, Roberts found himself in Cold Creek, Idaho. While there, he joined the Baptist church. In 1887, Roberts worked on the ranch of Buffalo Bill Cody near North Platte, Nebraska, where he continued to utilize his superb skills breaking horses.

During the spring of 1888, Roberts, using an alias, joined the Pinkerton Detective Agency. He remained in that position until early autumn, when he took a job with the Anti-Horsethief Association. As a member of the association, Roberts scouted much of the Red River valley in East Texas and Indian Territory, helping to rid the region of horsethieves. Like his previous job, this one lasted only a few months. During this time Roberts acquired a new nickname—the Hugo Kid— after the southeastern Oklahoma town of the same name. Later that same year, Roberts, again using an alias, went to work as a deputy for "Hanging Judge" Isaac C. Parker at Fort Smith, Arkansas. In 1889, Roberts, still calling himself the Hugo Kid, traveled to the annual cowboy roundup at Cheyenne, Wyoming, where he rode a wild horse called Cyclone and won a large purse.

By 1890, Roberts was tired of riding horses and decided to pursue a career as a boxer. He traveled to Cincinnati, Ohio, and trained for a while at a local gymnasium. As a fighter, however, he had little success. Roberts eventually returned to Oklahoma and resumed working with the Anti-Horsethief Association.

In 1892, Roberts took a job as a U.S. deputy marshal and spent most of his time investigating train holdups. In the process of attempting to thwart a train robbery, Roberts and another deputy encountered the Dalton gang. The deputy was killed and Roberts surrendered. He was recognized by one of the Daltons as Billy the Kid, and they let him go.

After quitting the marshal service, Roberts returned to breaking horses for a living and often competed in rodeos. In 1893, his riding skills earned him a job in Argentina. A large livestock company had shipped some Western-bred horses to the South American country and needed someone to show the natives how to work with them.

In 1894, after six months in Argentina, Roberts was hired to travel to the Shetland Islands, off the north coast of Scotland, to catch horses. After three months, Roberts and his crew captured about fifty head of the ponies. Following this, he returned to work once again for the Anti-Horsethief Association and was stationed along the Canadian River in Indian Territory.

While looking for some stolen horses, Roberts and his partner chanced on two dead men who had been killed by a deputy sheriff. Roberts recognized one of the dead as his cousin Oliver L. Roberts, who had run away from his Texas home years earlier. Before the man was buried, Roberts appropriated his identification and belongings, intending to return them to his family in Sulphur Springs, Texas. Weeks later when he arrived in Sulphur Springs, Oliver's mother, who had not seen her son in nearly a decade, mistook William Henry for him. From that time on, he used the alias of Ollie L. Roberts more than any other.

Late in 1894, Roberts rejoined the U.S. marshal service and served for three more years, taking time off now and then to ride with Wild West shows produced by Buffalo Bill and Pawnee Bill.

In 1895, Roberts went to El Paso, where he became reacquainted with some cattlemen he knew from "earlier times." Since Mexican president Porfirio Diaz was offering affordable terms on some excellent grazing land, Roberts, with nine other men, established a ranch in the state of Chihuahua, Mexico. Raising horses and mules, Roberts remained in Mexico until 1897.

In the spring of 1898, Roberts, once again calling himself the Hugo Kid, found himself in Claremore, Oklahoma, where he learned that Theodore Roosevelt was calling for volunteers for a regiment of Rough Riders. Intrigued, he traveled to Muskogee and enlisted, using another alias. From Muskogee, he was sent to San Antonio, Texas, where he trained for about three weeks before being shipped out to Cuba.

After landing in Cuba, Roberts was approached by a lieutenant who recognized him as the Texas Kid and made him a scout. Roberts's job, with that of fifteen other scouts, was to locate concentrations of the enemy and report back to headquarters.

The riding stock shipped to Cuba was difficult to handle. The lieutenant, knowing the reputation of the Texas Kid as a bronc rider, reassigned Roberts to handle the stock. A few officers resented the important responsibilities being given to the enlisted man and made their feelings known to him. Fistfights ensued and relationships were strained. Several days later, during a firefight with Cuban forces, some of the same officers were found shot in the back. Roberts and three other enlisted men were accused of killing the officers, were arrested, and were then court-martialed. Though no one was convicted, Roberts was sent back to the United States with an early discharge.

On arriving stateside, Roberts decided to return to his ranch in Chihuahua. In June 1899, President Diaz ordered the ranch seized, including all the horses and cattle. Soldiers were sent to confiscate the herds, but when they arrived, Roberts and his partners engaged them in a gun battle, killing about a dozen. Roberts was wounded several times.

Surviving soldiers rode for reinforcements, and a few days later the ranch house was surrounded by an estimated one thousand armed Mexican troops. With the American ranchers packing only what gear they could carry on a single horse, they fought their way through a weak section of the surround and fled for the border. Pursued along the way by the Mexican army, they finally crossed the Rio Grande near Del Rio, Texas, after thirteen days of hard riding.

In the spring of 1902, Roberts organized a Wild West show of his own and traveled parts of the western United States putting on performances. This lasted for almost two years. In 1904, he earned his living buying, selling, and trading cattle throughout Texas and Indian Territory.

In the company of two friends, Roberts returned to Mexico around 1907 and started a new ranch he named the Three Bar. Things went well until 1910, when the Mexican Revolution broke out. Roberts and his partners joined the army of Venustiano Carranza for a while, then signed on with revolutionary leader Pancho Villa, who subsequently used some of the horses from Roberts's ranch for his cavalry. As the Mexican Revolution was beginning to wind down in 1914, Roberts and his partners returned to the United States.

After settling down in his native Texas, Roberts married Mollie Brown of Coleman, a relative of the prominent Brown family for whom the town of Brownwood was named. Together, the two traveled around and lived in Texas, Oklahoma, and Arkansas while Roberts worked in the cattle and horse business. For a time, Roberts found employment in the oil fields of Oklahoma and again in Gladewater, Texas. While living in Gladewater, Roberts, again using an alias, took a job as a plainclothes policeman for the city force.

Mollie died in 1919. In 1925, Roberts remarried, this time to Louticia Ballard, who passed away in 1944. Shortly after being widowed a second time, Roberts met and married Melinda Allison. In their eighties, Roberts and Melinda were no longer able to hold down jobs and settled in Hamilton County, where the low cost of living enabled them to stretch their meager income. Here in 1948, Roberts was discovered by William V. Morrison.

On November 15, 1950, Morrison filed a petition for pardon with then New Mexico governor Thomas J. Mabry. The petition had been prepared by lawyers associated with the El Paso, Texas, law firm of Andress, Lipscomb, and Peticolas, and they specifically requested a full pardon for William Henry Roberts, as Billy the Kid, for the killing of sheriff William Brady on the streets of Lincoln on April 1, 1878.

After receiving Morrison's petition, Governor Mabry agreed to a meeting with Roberts and his representative in the chambers of the governor's mansion. Because of Roberts's apprehension about sitting down with the governor while under what he believed was a death sentence, Morrison assented to the meeting on the condition that it be private except for the appearance of some qualified historians. Mabry concurred.

Morrison and Roberts left El Paso for Santa Fe early on the morning of November 29. While stopping in Albuquerque for breakfast, Morrison was stunned to learn from reading a newspaper that the governor's meeting with Roberts was to be open to the public. When the two men arrived in Santa Fe, Morrison called the governor to protest.

Mabry apologized to Morrison over the telephone and explained that there had been an unauthorized leak to the press. An article concerning the visit that appeared in the previous day's issue of the *Santa Fe New Mexican* stated that the governor himself made a formal announcement of the meeting. In the article, Mabry stated that Oscar Garrett, the son of sheriff Pat Garrett, had been invited to sit in on the interview.

Over the telephone, Mabry agreed to a private hearing if Morrison and Roberts would come to the mansion around 9:30 A.M. and enter through the back door. Believing the governor was telling the truth this time, Morrison consented.

However, when Morrison and Roberts arrived at the mansion, they found dozens of people milling about the grounds, including reporters and photographers. For two days, the *Santa Fe New Mexican* had carried articles related to the pending visit by the man who claimed to be the outlaw Billy the Kid.

Morrison led a frightened Roberts through the back door of the mansion. Seconds later, Roberts, dressed in a fringed buckskin jacket, bandanna, cowboy boots, and cowboy hat, was met by the governor, who led him and Morrison to a large room where, according to Morrison, "many people were standing around near the walls." Once again, Governor Mabry had lied.

Roberts told Morrison that he was not feeling very well and was escorted to the governor's study where he lay down for twenty minutes. During this time, the governor remained with Roberts and engaged him in conversation.

When Roberts was feeling somewhat better, he and Morrison were led into a large dining room and seated at a big round table. At that point, the governor introduced Oscar and Jarvis Garrett, sons of the late Pat Garrett; and Cliff McKinney, the son of Thomas McKinney, one of the deputies with Garrett on the night Billy the Kid was allegedly killed. As he shook hands with the younger McKinney, Roberts's eyes dimmed as he related that once he and his father had been friends. "God bless you," he told Cliff McKinney.

Mabry introduced Arcadio Brady, the grandson of sheriff William Brady, whose grandfather Roberts allegedly murdered. He also introduced the sheriff of Eddy County, New Mexico; historians W. A. Keleher and Will Robinson of Santa Fe; and Paul A. Walter of Albuquerque. Among the invited guests was also Wilbur Coe, the son of Frank Coe and nephew of George Coe, both of whom participated in the Lincoln County War.

Morrison had an attorney from the Andress law firm call the governor and specifically request that Roberts not be "molested by reporters." Governor Mabry informed Morrison, however, that reporters would not be banned from the meeting and, in fact, would even be permitted to ask questions of Roberts. The governor, dishonoring his promise to Morrison for a private hearing, then opened up the meeting for questions. By now Roberts had grown apprehensive and feared he was going to be arrested. Like Morrison, he was upset by the deception and intimidation fostered by Mabry.

After Roberts fielded a few innocuous questions from McKinney, Governor Mabry turned to him and asked if he had been in Carlsbad recently. Roberts replied that he had passed through the town "about six months ago." Mabry, pointing to the Eddy County sheriff seated nearby, asked Roberts if he had seen him when he was there. Roberts said he had not.

In looking over the large room filled with reporters, photographers, and other visitors, Roberts spotted armed guards at the main doorway and grew visibly frightened. Later he told Morrison that he feared he was going to be arrested and was so upset and afraid he couldn't even remember the name of his own wife.

Historian Robinson asked Roberts several questions in what Morrison later described as a "memory test." A nervous Roberts had difficulty responding to Robinson's questions, explaining many of the events had taken place a long time ago. In turn, Roberts asked Robinson about some past event to which Robinson replied "that his memory was a bit hazy . . . after so many years." Robinson was, in fact, considerably younger than Roberts. Several of those in attendance asked Roberts questions about his place of birth, his mother's name, and certain events pertaining to the Lincoln County War. Roberts's answers often conflicted with the prevailing notion and published versions of Billy the Kid's life. As a result, according to Morrison, he was dismissed as having no credibility.

Mabry asked Roberts several odd questions. At one point, the governor inquired of him if he had a lot of girlfriends. Roberts replied that he had had "a good many girls" and that Garrett's sister-in-law Celsa Gutierrez was one of his favorites. When Mabry asked Roberts if he had ever been married, the old man replied that he didn't think the question had anything to do with the reason he was there.

Mabry then asked Roberts if he had ever stolen any cattle, to which Roberts replied a loud and defensive "No!" Mabry then asked Roberts how much money he expected to get out of the request for a pardon.

Before the meeting with Mabry, Morrison prepared a number of documents he intended to submit for consideration, documents providing evidence that William Henry Roberts was the outlaw Billy the Kid, but neither Mabry nor anyone else in the room wanted to see them. Instead, they continued asking trivial questions of the old man. When the meeting was adjourned, Roberts, looking pale and exhausted and feeling ill, asked if he could lie down once more. Ultimately, Roberts's request for a pardon was refused by the governor without a legal hearing and without the opportunity to present the accumulated evidence. Following the meeting, Mabry told a reporter that he didn't "think Roberts was Billy the Kid" and that he was "taking no action, now or ever, on this petition for a pardon."

After returning to El Paso, Morrison promised Roberts that he would continue working on the application for pardon, and Roberts returned home, a new residence in Hico, Texas.

Shortly after eating lunch on December 27, 1950, William Henry Roberts walked a few blocks from his house to the post office to mail a package for Melinda. As he passed the office of the Hico newspaper, his heart suddenly stopped beating, and the old man collapsed into the street, dead.

SIX

❖❖❖

Birth and Genealogy

The research process is a careful and diligent search, a studious inquiry or investigation aimed at discovery and interpretation, a balanced quest for truth. Research can lead to a revision of accepted notions and has withstood the test of time. Regarding the history of Billy the Kid and the Lincoln County War, those skilled in research design and procedure and those who have manifested keen and analytic insight into the issues include the late Dr. C. L. Sonnichsen, Dr. Richard Etulain, Frank Richard Prassel, Robert Utley, and Jon Tuska. Earlier historians include Maurice Garland Fulton and William A. Keleher, each of whom made important contributions to the topics during the 1950s and 1960s.

The claim that William Henry Roberts was Billy the Kid rocked the world of Western American outlaw and lawman history when it was formally made in 1950. What was likewise stunning was the claim that another young man was mistaken for the Kid and was shot by Pat Garrett in Pete Maxwell's bedroom the night of July 14, 1881. If true, it will cause history to be rewritten.

The actual place and date of Billy the Kid's birth, as well as his genealogy, have long eluded researchers. The first written account of the Kid's birth was in the Garrett–Upson book *The Authentic Life of Billy the Kid*: "William Bonney, the hero of this history, was born in the city of New York, November 23, 1859." No one knows where Garrett or Upson learned this bit of information, but it has served to send researchers to New York City to attempt to verify the statement, all unsuccessfully.

There are two possible explanations for the Garrett–Upson attribution to New York City as the Kid's birthplace. First, Billy the Kid himself may have told such a thing to the sheriff. Garrett and the Kid knew each other and were on speaking terms. A habit of many men in the West, particularly those who had a past they wanted to hide, was

51

to claim names and hometowns other than their own. Billy the Kid employed at least three aliases while living in Lincoln County—Henry Antrim, Henry McCarty, and Billy Bonney—and it is known that he offered different versions of his origins. In addition to the hypothetical New York City connection, the 1880 census records for Fort Sumner, New Mexico, listed the vital statistics of one "William Bonny," who lived next to the residence of Charlie Bowdre and named his place of birth as Missouri.

Second, according to researcher Frederick Nolan, Ash Upson (who coauthored *Authentic Life*) possessed little credibility. The statement about the Kid's birthdate may have been one of Upson's own creations. *Authentic Life*, says writer J. C. Dykes, "is responsible for the perpetuation of unverified tales about his early life." If Upson had access to any truths, maintains Dykes, he laid them aside "in favor of trying to outdo the writers of those 'yellow-covered cheap novels.'" In *Pat Garrett: The Story of a Western Lawman*, author Leon Metz refers to Upson's writings about Billy the Kid as "blatant falsehoods." Also important to note here is that the date of birth that Garrett–Upson provided for the Kid—November 23, 1859—happened to be Upson's birth date. The notion that Billy the Kid was born in New York City was, in all probability, made up either by Garrett or Uspon or by the Kid himself.

One of the most comprehensive books to date about the outlaw is *Billy the Kid: A Short and Violent Life* by Robert M. Utley, a compilation of extant material pertaining to the Kid. He states that "the Kid's origins are shrouded in mystery and buffeted by controversy. A corps of diligent researchers has tracked him in census records, city directories, baptismal and marriage registers, newspapers, and other sources. Discoveries have been tantalizingly suggestive but rarely conclusive." Utley then quotes research by Jack DeMattos and Donald Cline that attempts to prove that the Kid was born illegitimate in New York City on September 7, 1859; that his Christian name was Henry; that he was a product of the Irish slums; that his mother's first name may have been Catherine; and that his father's name may have been McCarty.

In *The Lincoln County War: A Documentary History*, author Frederick Nolan writes that over the years others who claimed to know Billy the Kid have supported the proposition that he was born in New York, "but the strength of their testimony is diluted by the fact that they could have read it elsewhere first and then 'remembered' it." Nolan notes that the Garrett–Upson book, as well as dozens of newspaper reports published soon after the death of Billy the Kid, stated that New York was the outlaw's birthplace. The fact was that no one knew the truth.

Historians cannot agree on the place and date of the Kid's birth, simply because no one has found any compelling evidence for the claims. An organization called the Billy the Kid Outlaw Gang is offering five hundred dollars "to the first person who finds irrefutable proof of Henry McCarty's birth, his father, and where he was born." No one has yet claimed the reward.

In contrast, William Henry Roberts, alias Billy the Kid, claimed he was born in Buffalo Gap, Texas, on December 31, 1859. According to his statements, his mother's maiden name was Mary Adeline Dunn and his father was James Henry Roberts, both of whom were from Lexington, Kentucky. Roberts states that he was taken in by his aunt Catherine Bonney following the death of his mother when he was about three years old. Catherine Bonney was Mary Adeline's half sister.

While a great deal of time and effort clearly went into the study of historical New York City records to establish a Billy the Kid connection, it appears that the researchers forced a conclusion where none existed. The documentation cited by DeMattos and Cline revolves around the residents of New York City's Irish Fourth Ward during the late 1850s and early 1860s. At the time, this area was occupied by thousands of Irish immigrants. According to Nolan, some thirteen thousand tenements were crowded into this section, which covered approximately eighty-three acres. The 1870 census lists the population of the Fourth Ward as 10,546 natives and 13,292 foreigners. The chances of finding Irish residents named McCarty in this part of New York would be similar to finding someone named Smith in Los Angeles. It represents a giant leap of faith to conclude that a child with the common Irish name of Henry born to a woman with the common Irish name of Catherine and a man with the common Irish surname of McCarty is none other than Billy the Kid. Utley writes that the question of birth, as it is advanced by DeMattos and Cline, is "complicated by the sloppy record keeping of the times and the superabundance, in New York . . . of McCartys, McCarthys, and McCartneys named Patrick, Michael, Henry, Joseph, and Catherine."

According to author Nolan, the "inescapable conclusion is that the only birth that can be stated to be even probably that of a participant in the story of Billy the Kid is that of Joseph McCarty, and even that is open to considerable doubt." Nolan states that there is an "absence of definitive documentation" regarding the New York birth claim.

Roberts maintained he was raised by an aunt—his mother's half sister Catherine Bonney. The origin of the name Bonney has eluded and confounded Billy the Kid researchers—they have never been able to determine where it came from.

Roberts had an answer, and his explanation was subsequently supported by a genealogy found in a Roberts family Bible in the possession of his widow Melinda. According to additional genealogy records provided to Frederic Bean by Bill Allison and descendants of James Henry's brother Henry Oliver, William Henry Roberts's aunt Catherine Bonney, born in 1829, was the daughter of a man named Bonney, whose first name was not recorded in the Bible, and an unnamed wife. Following the death of husband Bonney, the widow remarried to William Dunn and bore Mary Adeline, Catherine Bonney's half sister.

The genealogy shows that Catherine Bonney first married a man named Michael McCarty, who died while fighting in the War between the States. The two had a son, Joseph. Catherine subsequently married William Antrim in Santa Fe, New Mexico, in 1873, bringing to the union her son Joseph and her nephew William Henry. Catherine Antrim, née Bonney, raised William Henry as if he were her own son.

Roberts's claims, supported by the family history found in his Bible, are significant for several reasons: first, they account for the source of three principal aliases used by Roberts while living in Lincoln County—Henry Antrim, Henry McCarty, and Billy Bonney—and they do so in a logical and verifiable manner; second, the records show William Henry Roberts to be approximately the same age Billy the Kid was presumed to be; and third, they are derived from verifiable records.

In addition, Roberts's Texas origins are also supportive of other aspects of the life of Billy the Kid: his facility with Spanish, his riding and horse-breaking skills, and his competence with firearms. He manifested these abilities at a relatively young age, and such activities were not common in New York City's Irish Fourth Ward. The west-central Texas location of Hamilton County, Texas, offers a plausible alternative.

The traditional history as it relates to the birth and genealogy of the Kid lacks cogency and has never been verified. William Henry Roberts's explanations provide a strong and convincing case.

SEVEN

✦✦✦

¿Quién Es? *A Reexamination of the Shooting at Fort Sumner*

The events presented here immediately leading up to and including the night of July 14, 1881, are drawn principally from the published narratives provided by two of the lawmen who were present—sheriff Pat Garrett, the author of *The Authentic Life of Billy the Kid*, and deputy sheriff John W. Poe, who wrote *The Death of Billy the Kid*—as well as tape-recorded recollections of William Henry Roberts made in 1949.

During the first week of July 1881, citizens of Lincoln County and the surrounding area were aware that Billy the Kid was staying at Fort Sumner following his dramatic escape from jail. Even the *Las Vegas Gazette* (May 19, 1881) reported on his temporary residency, stating that the Kid "is not far from Fort Sumner and has not left that neighborhood since he rode over from Lincoln after making his break."

Before long, Sheriff Garrett learned of the Kid's hiding place. Garrett was surprised that the Kid had not fled far and fast, and in *Authentic Life* he wrote, "It seemed incredible that he should linger in the Territory."

Garrett was determined to go after the Kid. On July 10, in the company of deputies John Poe and Thomas McKinney, the sheriff left Roswell for Fort Sumner. On the evening of July 13, the three men made camp near the mouth of Taliban Creek, located just below Fort Sumner. At the time, the town claimed a population of approximately 250 residents, most of whom were Mexicans and who sympathized with the Kid. Since no one in Fort Sumner knew Poe, the deputy rode into town to try to gather some information about the outlaw. Around ten o'clock in the morning of July 14, Poe entered Fort Sumner, where he was immediately greeted with suspicion.

Claiming to be a miner from White Oaks, New Mexico, Poe bought a round of drinks in the saloon and ate lunch in a restaurant, all the while trying to learn something of the whereabouts of the Kid. He had no luck. In *The Death of Billy the Kid*, Poe writes that it was evident how many of them were on the alert and how there was a very tense situation in Fort Sumner on that day. Poe believed that since "the Kid was at that time hiding in one of the houses there, and if the object of my visit had become known, I should have stood no chance for my life whatsoever."

Unable to learn anything in town, Poe rode seven miles north to the ranch of Milnor Rudolph, an acquaintance of Garrett and a friend of the Kid. Arriving in the evening, Poe gave Rudolph a letter of introduction from Garrett and was invited to take lodging for the night.

Following dinner, Poe commented that he had heard the Kid was hiding in or near Fort Sumner. Rudolph, appearing nervous, replied that he had heard such reports but did not believe them. In his book, Poe stated that Rudolph told him that the Kid was "too shrewd to be caught lingering in that part of the country with a price on his head and knowing that officers of the law were diligently seeking him." Poe deduced that Rudolph was "in mortal terror of the Kid and, on account of this fear, was very reluctant to say anything whatever about him."

After Poe finally explained the purpose of his visit to Rudolph, the host grew more nervous than ever and reiterated his reasons for believing that the Kid was not in that part of New Mexico. Poe concluded that Rudolph knew exactly where the Kid was hiding but was so afraid of the outlaw that he provided misleading statements to the lawman.

Instead of remaining at Rudolph's residence, Poe returned to Garrett and McKinney at the Taiban Creek campsite. After reporting to the sheriff, Poe was told by Garrett that he had "little confidence in our being able to accomplish the object of this trip." Garrett did say, however, that he knew a woman in Fort Sumner who could likely tell them where the Kid might be found. Garrett was probably speaking of his brother-in-law's wife, Celsa Gutierrez, wife of Saval Gutierrez and known to have been a girlfriend of Billy the Kid.

About nine o'clock that evening, the three lawmen arrived at a peach orchard just north of town. Under a full moon, according to Poe, they waited until eleven o'clock, at which time Garrett suggested they leave town "without letting anyone know we had been there in search of the Kid."

THREE VERSIONS OF THE SHOOTING

Instead of leaving, Poe proposed they go to the residence of Pete Maxwell, a leading citizen and property owner of Fort Sumner, and ask him if he knew where the Kid was hiding. Garrett agreed and led Poe and McKinney on foot from the orchard to Maxwell's residence, once an officers' quarters during the days when troops were garrisoned at the fort.

According to Garrett, the three lawmen approached a cluster of houses where Fort Sumner residents lived, and they soon heard the sound of voices conversing in Spanish. Garrett, Poe, and McKinney concealed themselves and listened but were too far away to hear words or distinguish voices. "Soon a man arose from the ground, in full view," wrote Garrett, "but too far away to recognize. He wore a broad-brimmed hat, a dark vest and pants, and was in his shirt sleeves."

After speaking a few words, the man walked to the fence, jumped it, and proceeded toward rancher Maxwell's house. "Little as we then suspected it, this man was the Kid," concluded Garrett. After the man left the orchard, the three lawmen retreated a short distance and, selecting a different route, approached Maxwell's house from the opposite direction.

William Henry Roberts recalled that the night was dark but that there was enough moonlight to make shadows. Roberts and his partner, Billy Barlow, rode up to Jesus Silva's house in the dark. "We'd been staying out at the Yerby Ranch, laying low for a while," stated Roberts. "Word was all around . . . that Pat Garrett and a posse was after me. Pat's wife was a sister to my friend Saval Gutierrez, and Saval told me that Pat was after me—he heard it from his sister. Things were mighty hot in Lincoln County for me right about then, but I wasn't running from it. I meant to have a talk with Pat Garrett and set things straight between us if I could. We used to be friends."

Roberts and Barlow hid their horses in a nearby barn and walked up to Silva's back door. Barlow exhibited some nervousness about being in Fort Sumner, knowing that the sheriff was looking for the Kid. When Roberts tapped on Silva's back door with the barrel of his revolver, the friend let them in, happy to see them. Roberts told Silva that he and Barlow were hungry and that they had "been out in the hills all day, scouting around Fort Sumner for any sign of Garrett and his posse."

As Silva ushered them inside, he told them he had nothing but cold beans. Barlow grimaced and said he needed some meat, that he and the Kid had been living on little more than beans and tortillas for a week. Barlow asked Silva if he had any beef. Silva shrugged and told him that Maxwell had recently killed and butchered a steer and a hindquarter was hanging on his back porch. Silva suggested Barlow go cut some strips while he started the fire.

Roberts said, "I didn't like the idea. We were safe inside the house with our horses hidden in the barn. I figured we ought to leave things like they were until morning and I said so." Roberts urged Barlow not to leave the house.

In the meantime, Garrett, Poe, and McKinney arrived at Maxwell's house. Poe recalled Garrett leading them to Maxwell's room near the corner of the building and telling him and McKinney to wait on the porch while he spoke with the rancher. Poe wrote that Garrett "stepped onto the porch and entered Maxwell's room through the open door, while McKinney and myself stopped on the outside. McKinney squatted on the outside of the fence, and I sat on the edge of the porch in the small open gateway leading from the street onto the porch." Up to this point, Deputy Poe had never before seen Billy the Kid, or for that matter Pete Maxwell. McKinney may have been acquainted with the outlaw.

In Silva's house, Roberts was trying to get Barlow to calm down. "Barlow was in a foul mood," he said. "We'd been on the dodge since I broke out of jail. He had his mind made up to have beefsteak, and I couldn't talk him out of it." After telling Silva and the Kid he was sick and tired of eating beans, he borrowed a butcher knife and said he was going over to Maxwell's. As Barlow started for the door, Roberts "had this crazy feeling that he hadn't ought to go, like somebody whispered in my ear that it was all wrong and there might be some trouble out there." Roberts told Barlow to stay in the house, that they could go after some beef in the morning, but "he went out anyway, like he hadn't heard a word I said to him."

Garrett wrote that around midnight he entered Maxwell's room and found the rancher in bed. "I walked to the head of the bed and sat down on it, beside him, near the pillow. I asked him as to the where-abouts of the Kid, but he did not know whether he had left or not."

Poe recalled that "it was not more than thirty seconds after Garrett had entered Maxwell's room, when my attention was at-tracted, from where I sat in the little gateway, to a man approaching me on the inside of and along the fence, some forty of fifty steps away. I observed that he was only partially dressed and was both bareheaded and barefooted, or rather, had only socks on his feet, and it seemed to me he was fastening his trousers as he came toward me at a very brisk walk."

Poe was convinced that Maxwell's was the last place Billy the Kid would try to hide. Not expecting anyone to be out that time of night, the deputy "was entirely off my guard, the thought coming into my mind that the man approaching was either Maxwell or some guest of his who might have been staying there. He came on until he was almost within arm's length of where I sat, before he saw me, as I was partially concealed from his view by the post of the gate."

According to Poe, the newcomer, on spotting him "covered me with his six-shooter as quick as lightning, sprang onto the porch, calling out in Spanish *¿Quién es?* [Who is it?]—at the same time backing away from me toward the door through which Garrett only a few seconds before had passed, repeating his query, 'Who is it?' in Spanish several times."

At this, Poe stood up and advanced toward the stranger, telling him not to be alarmed and that no one was going to hurt him, all the time not having the least suspicion "that this was the very man we were looking for." Poe stepped forward and attempted to reassure the newcomer, but the man "backed up into the doorway of Maxwell's room, where he halted for a moment, his body concealed by the thick adobe wall at the side of the doorway, from whence he put out his head and asked in Spanish for the fourth or fifth time who I was. I was within a few feet of him when he disappeared into the room."

Garrett claimed that "a man sprang quickly into the door, looking back, and called twice in Spanish, 'Who comes there?'" Receiving no reply, the man entered the room. Garrett wrote that he was not wearing a hat and that "from his step I could perceive he was either barefooted or in his stocking feet, and held a revolver in his right hand and a butcher knife in his left."

Garrett claimed that the man came directly toward him but, before reaching the bed, whispered to Maxwell, asking him who the men outside were. Maxwell made no reply, and Garrett thought for a moment that the visitor might be Pete's brother-in-law Manuel Abreau, who had seen Poe and McKinney outside and wanted to know their business.

Garrett said, "The intruder came close to me, leaned both hands on the bed, his right hand almost touching my knee, and asked, in a low tone: 'Who are they, Pete?' At the same instant Maxwell whispered to me. 'That's him!' Simultaneously the Kid must have seen, or felt, the presence of a third person at the head of the bed. He raised his pistol, a self cocker, within a foot of my breast. Retreating rapidly across the room he cried: *¿Quién es? ¿Quién es?* Who's that? Who's that? All this occurred in a moment. Quickly as possible I drew my revolver and fired, threw my body aside, and fired again. The second shot was useless; the Kid fell dead. He never spoke. A struggle or two, a little strangling sound as he gasped for breath, and the Kid was with his many victims."

Poe remembered that an instant after the man disappeared inside the room, he heard a voice inquire in a sharp tone, asking Maxwell about the men outside. An instant later, "a shot was fired in the room, followed immediately by what everyone within hearing distance thought were two other shots." Poe insisted, however, that only two shots were fired and maintained that the third report was caused by "the rebound of the second bullet, which had struck the adobe wall and rebounded against the headboard of the wooden bedstead." From where he stood near the doorway, Poe heard "a groan and one or two gasps . . . as of someone dying in the room."

Roberts was visiting with Silva and watching him make preparations for a meal when he heard the shots coming from the direction of Maxwell's place. He withdrew one of his forty-fours and ran through the door, trying to see in the dark. He said that two more shots rang out from the shadows near the Maxwell house but that he was unable to locate a target at which to return fire.

Immediately following Garrett's shots, Maxwell plunged over the foot of the bed onto the floor, dragging the bedclothes with him. Garrett walked to the door, where he found Poe and McKinney awaiting an explanation. Maxwell rushed out the door and onto the porch, bumping into Poe, only to be met by drawn revolvers. Maxwell cried out, "Don't shoot, don't shoot."

Poe remembered Garrett exiting the room, coming close to him near the wall at the side of the door and saying, "That was the Kid who came in there, and I think I have got him." Poe replied, "Pat, the Kid would not come to this place; you have shot the wrong man." According to Poe, "Garrett seemed to be in doubt himself as to whom he had shot, but quickly spoke up and said, 'I am sure that was him, for I know his voice too well to be mistaken.'" At the time, Garrett's comment relieved Poe of "considerable apprehension, as I felt almost certain that someone whom we did not want had been killed."

Roberts ran toward Maxwell's porch. He heard another gunshot and was stuck by a bullet in the jaw. He stumbled and kept on running, a broken tooth rolling around on his tongue. Tasting blood, he spit the tooth out and emptied his revolver at the shadow where he last spotted the muzzleflash. From the corner of his eye, he saw a body lying on the back porch. "I knew it had to be Barlow," he said. "My partner had walked right into a trap, and the trap had likely been set for me."

Roberts pulled his other .44 and ran toward the porch to check on Barlow but ran right into a wall of gunfire. "I knew I wasn't going to make it to my partner. Too many guns were shooting at me. I didn't have a chance." Roberts turned and ran toward a fence at the rear of Maxwell's yard. As he dove behind it, a bullet caught him in the left shoulder. After landing hard on the far side, and with the echo of gunshots ringing in his ears, he staggered into an alley that ran behind the house, firing his revolver over his shoulder until it clicked empty. His mouth and shoulder were bleeding, and he lost track of where he was, but he had the presence of mind to get away from Maxwell's before they killed him. Roberts heard a shout and another gunshot.

> Something passed across my forehead like a hot branding iron. I was stunned. I lost my footing and fell on my face in the darkness. I knew I was hurt bad and I wondered if I would make it out of this scrape alive. I forced myself up again, wiping the blood from my eyes with a shirtsleeve as I stumbled headlong down the alley. I didn't know how bad the head wound was, only that it was bleeding and I couldn't see. It wouldn't matter if they found me in the alley just then, they were bent on killing me, to be sure. If I fell again, I knew they'd find me and finish the job, so I kept running down the alley as hard as I could, barely able to see where I was going.

Roberts heard shouting behind him, then some men arguing over something, but he was too frightened to care. He was certain they were searching for him. The wound to his head left him staggering, senseless, and he kept running down the alley, trying to get away. Blood was pouring into his eyes and he was unable to see.

Roberts ran past a little adobe shack just down the alley from Maxwell's. "I suppose all the shooting woke everybody up, because a door opened just a crack when I ran behind the adobe, and I could see a lantern light spilling from the doorway across the alley. I stumbled toward the light, not knowing what else to do. I needed help, and the open door was the only place I could find, hurt like I was." A Mexican woman pulled him inside. On seeing the blood on Roberts's face, she threw her hands over her mouth, closed the door quickly, and helped him to a chair.

Meanwhile, Garrett was telling Poe and McKinney that he shot the Kid. The deputies asked the sheriff if he might have shot the wrong man, but Garrett replied, "I had made no blunder, that I knew the Kid's voice too well to be mistaken. The Kid was entirely unknown to either of them." The three lawmen entered the room, examined the body, and discovered that a bullet had struck the unfortunate man just above the heart. Garrett claimed, "We examined his pistol—a self-cocker, caliber forty-one."

Poe recalled that Maxwell obtained "an old-fashioned tallow candle from his mother's room" and placed it on the outside window sill. "This enabled us to get a view from the inside, where we saw a man lying stretched out upon his back dead, in the middle of the room, with a six-shooter lying in his right hand and a butcher knife at his left." On examining the body, Poe said they "found it to be that of Billy the Kid. Garrett's first shot had penetrated the breast just above the heart."

In the room of the old woman, Roberts sleeved the blood from his eyes and saw her reloading his Colts. Blood was oozing from his mouth where the bullet hit his jaw, and his shoulder was throbbing with pain from the slug that had passed through it. He began to lose consciousness again and cried out for help. He asked the old woman to put something on the wounds to keep them from bleeding. He told her, "I've got to get the hell away from here before they find me. My horse is in Jesus' barn—I need someone to saddle it for me. They shot my partner. Please help me." Before the woman could answer, Roberts passed out.

Within a short time after the shooting, a number of the Fort Sumner residents gathered near Pete Maxwell's bedroom, some of them, according to Poe, bewailing the death of their friend. "Several women pleaded for permission to take charge of the body, which we allowed them to do. They carried it across the yard to a carpenter shop, where it was laid out on a workbench; the women placed lighted candles around it according to their ideas of properly conducting a 'wake' for the dead."

Poe said the three lawmen spent the remainder of the night on the Maxwell premises, constantly on guard "as we were expecting to be attacked by friends of the dead man." The following morning, wrote Poe, Garrett sent for a justice of the peace, who held an inquest over the body, "the verdict of the jury being such as to justify the killing, and later on the same day, the body was buried in the military burying ground at Fort Sumner."

Two hours before dawn, Roberts regained consciousness. When he woke up, the old woman was placing beef tallow on his forehead to stop the bleeding. He saw another woman in the room, and when his vision cleared, he recognized Celsa Gutierrez. When Roberts inquired about Garrett and his posse, Celsa told him they were still inside Maxwell's house, that they were afraid to come out in the dark, believing that friends of the Kid would try to shoot them. Celsa said the lawmen would not leave the house until daylight.

Celsa confirmed what Roberts had already guessed. He believed that "Garrett and his posse had been laying for me over at Maxwell's. They knew Pete and I were friends and that I'd stop by to see him if I was in this country." Celsa told Roberts she had sent for his friend Frank Lobato, that he was at that moment saddling two horses and would bring them to the alley when she informed him the Kid was able to ride.

Celsa told Roberts that Pat Garrett was telling everyone that the Kid was dead. She said they dragged Barlow's body inside the house and were saying that it was Billy the Kid. She also informed him that several men from town were dispatched by the sheriff to the Fort Sumner cemetery to dig a grave by lantern light. Celsa said Deluvina Maxwell was carrying on and crying but that she knew Garrett killed the wrong man. Roberts said that Celsa told him, "She is pretending, going along with what the men are saying. Your partner looks very much like you in the dark except for his beard. His eyes are blue, like yours, Billy. Pat says they will bury the body in the morning. If the coffin is closed, who will guess that you are not inside it?"

Roberts was confused about what Celsa told him and wondered if he heard it correctly. Was Garrett, he wondered, trying to pass off Barlow's body as his? He and Garrett had once been friends, and he knew that the sheriff had to know the body wasn't his. So why, he considered, was Garrett telling everybody he had killed Billy the Kid?

Celsa eventually left by the back door. The Mexican woman tied a bandage around Roberts's shoulder and placed more tallow on his forehead. Minutes later, Roberts heard horses arriving at the side of the adobe. He hobbled through the door and around the corner to where Frank Lobato was waiting with two saddled horses. Lobato helped Roberts into the saddle, and the two rode quietly away from the adobe, keeping the house between them and Maxwell's. When they were away from town, Roberts thought again of what Celsa told him. Garrett was trying to pass off Barlow's body as that of Billy the Kid. Roberts wondered how Garrett figured to get away with it.

Garrett knew by now that he had killed the wrong man in the dark. Billy Barlow looked a lot like him, the same size and general description, with similar blue eyes. But in the daylight, pondered Roberts, people who knew Billy the Kid would know they had the wrong body. Roberts was confused and decided that Garrett realized his mistake and was going to try to collect the reward that was out on the outlaw Billy the Kid.

CONTRADICTIONS AND INCONSISTENCIES

Milnor Rudolph and the Kid were friends. Rudolph probably appeared nervous to Deputy Poe because he knew exactly where the Kid was hiding and was intent on protecting him. Though Poe presumed that Rudolph was withholding information, writer Alfred Adler suggests, "Rudolph and the nativos cannot be dissociated from the other inhabitants of Fort Sumner who were . . . eager to hide the Kid." Once Garrett decided, perhaps unilaterally, that the man he killed was the Kid, continues Adler, "what a wonderful opportunity for the coroner's jury . . . to save their idol by making the death official!"

The only surviving witnesses to the shooting of the man in Pete Maxwell's bedroom were Garrett, who insisted he pulled the trigger, and Maxwell. Deputies Poe and McKinney were within a few feet of the room but were participants only in the events following the actual killing. Maxwell has contributed very little to explaining what took place in the room. McKinney likewise remained silent about the events of that night for most of his life, but years later made comments that cast doubt on the versions offered by Garrett and Poe.

Ultimately, all that is "known" about the killing is what has been written by Garrett in *Authentic Life* and by Poe in *The Death of Billy the Kid*. An examination of these two published accounts reveals a few similarities relative to the events of that night but also some glaring contradictions.

Garrett writes that shortly after arriving at Maxwell's estate, he and the deputies spotted a man in the orchard that he claims was Billy the Kid, but he never explains how he knew it to be so. More to the point, how could he have known it was the Kid, if it were? Garrett then wrote, "The Kid, by me unrecognized." Did the sheriff recognize Billy the Kid or not? Garrett contradicts himself.

All Garrett based his recognition on was the mode of apparel worn by the subject, but the young man who entered Maxwell's room was clothed in completely different garb. Poe, however, never mentions the incident, an important one if it happened at all. If Garrett's account were true, then such a dramatic moment would have been recalled and noted by Poe. Could it be that it never happened and that Garrett, or Upson, made it up?

After Poe suggested to Garrett that he might have killed the wrong man, the sheriff replied that he did not err and that "he knew the Kid's voice too well to be mistaken." But according to Garrett, the man who entered Maxwell's bedroom was whispering or speaking in low tones. When Garrett claimed he knew the Kid's voice, did he mean his whisper? In spite of Garrett's claimed intimacy with the Kid's voice, he still had to ask Maxwell who the newcomer was. On the subject of the Kid's voice, Garrett contradicts himself again and erodes his credibility even further.

Garrett stated that, just before the shooting, "a man sprang quickly into the door" to Maxwell's room. Yet, Poe wrote that the stranger "backed into the doorway . . . halted for a moment . . . put out his head and asked in Spanish for the fourth or fifth time who I was. I was within a few feet of him when he disappeared into the room." Here are two remarkably different versions of the same event from two men who allegedly witnessed it together.

Maxwell's bedroom was probably not very large. The two men inside the room—Garrett and Maxwell, one or both of them nervous and alert—would have been aware of the appearance of a stranger as a result of the conversation taking place between him and Deputy Poe only a few feet away. It remains difficult to believe that Garrett and Maxwell were not aware of the arrival of the newcomer who was speaking to Poe and backing into the open doorway. Yet Garrett insists that the man "sprang quickly" into the room. Did he back in, or did he spring? These two actions would be hard to confuse. Furthermore, why would a man who manifested nervousness at the presence of the two deputies spring into a dark room without knowing who was inside? Either Garrett or Poe or both must be mistaken.

Garrett also stated that it was so dark in Maxwell's bedroom that the intruder came within inches, close enough to touch, yet the sheriff could not see him. However, Garrett claimed that, only a moment earlier, he could see a butcher knife and a pistol in the newcomer's hands. Yet Maxwell could apparently see in the dark well enough to identify the Kid for the sheriff. In *Billy the Kid: A Handbook*, author Jon Tuska refers to this entire sequence as a Garrett–Upson fantasy.

There were other significant contradictions in the published writings of Garrett and Poe. In *Authentic Life*, Garrett states that he learned that

the Kid was in the area from a letter that had been written to him by a
rancher named Brazil, who claimed to be hiding from the outlaw. Poe,
in his book, writes that it was he who learned about the Kid's where-
abouts from a Texas man and that he, in turn, communicated the information to Garrett, who was reluctant to believe him. Once again, two
entirely different versions of the same event exist.

Even the similarities in the accounts of the two men are trouble-
some. For instance, in *Authentic Life*, Garrett states that he had not
blundered, that he "knew the Kid's voice too well to be mistaken."
This is an odd statement coming only moments after Garrett had to
ask Maxwell who the newcomer was. In *The Death of Billy the Kid*,
published thirty-eight years later, Poe, after telling Garrett that he
shot the wrong man, quotes the sheriff as responding, "I am sure that
was him, for I know his voice too well to be mistaken."

Poe's manuscript on the death of the Kid, originally published in
Wide World magazine and coming nearly four decades after the
shooting, seemed quite precise regarding Garrett's statement from
that long-ago night. Was Poe's memory so keen that he remembered the sheriff's exact words? Or is it more likely that his recollections of that night were influenced by his reading of the
Garrett–Upson account?

And why, after disagreeing with Garrett that night on who was actually killed, did Poe finally come around to supporting the sheriff's
version? The answer may lie in the fact that both men were Masons
and were committed to a fraternal bond relative to collaborating
their stories.

There are even more inconsistencies when Poe's published account
is compared with those of others. According to Poe, when he peered
into Maxwell's room, he "saw a man lying on his back, dead, in the
middle of the room." Yet Jesus Silva tells Miguel Antonio Otero in *The
Real Billy the Kid: With New Light on the Lincoln County War* that
when he entered Maxwell's bedroom moments after the shooting, the
dead man was "stretched out, face down." Silva claimed that after
entering the room, "we turned him over."

Poe also claims that the body was removed from the room "a very
short time after the shooting" and carried "across the yard to a carpenter shop, where it was laid out on a workbench, the women placing lighted candles around it according to their ideas of properly
conducting a 'wake' for the dead."

In stark contradiction to Poe is Charles Frederick Rudulph, in his
book *Los Billitos: The Story of Billy the Kid and His Gang*, who

writes that Milner Rudolph conducted the proceedings of the coroner's jury on the morning of July 15 in Pete Maxwell's bedroom with the body still lying on the floor. In *Billy the Kid: A Short and Violent Life*, author Utley also writes that the body was removed the day following the killing and after the Rudolph-conducted inquest. Once again, radically different versions of the same event.

Then there is the question of the gun. Both Garrett and Poe claimed that the man who entered Maxwell's bedroom carried a .41-caliber pistol in his right hand and a butcher knife in his left. According to author Donald Cline, Poe later claimed the pistol was a .38 Colt double-action and that he never saw it until Garrett brought it from the room of Celsa Gutierrez. If the stranger were the Kid, why was he carrying a caliber of pistol he was never known to use? When the Kid escaped from the Lincoln County jail, he took two .44s from the armory.

Did the man Garrett claimed to be the Kid carry a gun at all? In *Violence in Lincoln County*, author William H. Keleher writes that the person who walked into Maxwell's bedroom had only a knife. Utley writes that a "belief persists that Billy was armed only with a butcher knife" and that "Garrett and Poe had reason to want the world to believe that Billy carried a pistol." In *History of the Lincoln County War*, Maurice G. Fulton states that the man carried only a butcher knife. Former New Mexico governor Miguel Otero, who interviewed Fort Sumner residents Francisco Lobato, Jesus Silva, and Deluvina Maxwell, learned that the man shot by Garrett was not carrying a pistol when he was killed.

Was a pistol placed in the right hand of the dead man after the shooting to make it appear he was armed? Garrett, who had high political ambitions, must have realized that shooting an unarmed man would not look good. If indeed a pistol were provided, a so-called drop weapon, whoever did so made a mistake and gave the dead man a gun Billy the Kid never used.

There are more inconsistencies. There is no agreement on whether there were two shots fired or three; there is disagreement on whether the body of the slain man was inside or outside the room. Author Nolan contends that *Authentic Life* was written to make Garrett look good, that it was necessary to "exaggerate the Kid's recklessness, his gunfighting skills, his murderous nature," all designed to "present Garrett as a courageous lawman."

Odelia Bernice Finley Johnson, great-granddaughter of Lucien B. Maxwell, once related an account by Deluvina Maxwell, one of Pete Maxwell's workers, that conflicts with positions taken by Garrett and

Poe. According to Johnson, Garrett and the two deputies were afraid to reenter the room after the shooting, believing that the stranger was only wounded and lying in wait for them. After roundly cursing Garrett, Deluvina grabbed a candle and walked into the bedroom—perhaps the first to do so—to render aid to the victim.

The question *¿Quién es?* asked of Poe, McKinney, and Maxwell by the stranger provides another provocative element. William Henry Roberts maintains that the man who went to Maxwell's room was a friend named Billy Barlow. Author Sonnichsen learned from Roberts that Barlow may have been half Mexican. If Billy the Kid, an Anglo, had entered Maxwell's bedroom and encountered the resident who spoke excellent English, why would he question him in Spanish? It is likely that a person of Mexican heritage would be more inclined to speak Spanish than English.

More important, if the man who approached Maxwell's room that night was the Kid, sentenced to hang, living on the run, and hiding out because of the posted reward for his capture, he would hardly have paused long enough to ask Poe and McKinney *¿Quién es?* The Kid had been informed that a posse was on his trail and that several citizens of Fort Sumner had alerted him to the presence of Garrett. The Kid would have surely been more careful than to have simply blundered up to Maxwell's house on a night that he knew there were lawmen looking for him. Even Poe told Garrett, "The Kid would not come to this place."

The fugitive, having already killed Olinger and Bell, would most likely have shot Poe and McKinney. According to Poe, there was a full moon—light enough for anyone to see that the two men hanging around outside of Maxwell's bedroom were not residents of Fort Sumner. Strangers were certainly enough to arouse the suspicion of a wanted man who knew he was being pursued; unless, of course, the man who went to Maxwell's room was not Billy the Kid.

There is yet another consideration. If Billy the Kid approached the house that night, McKinney might have recognized him because the two allegedly knew each other. In the light of the full moon, McKinney could see that the newcomer was not the Kid, so he simply let him pass. Why, then, didn't McKinney say anything when Garrett was intent on identifying the dead man as Billy the Kid? McKinney, young and inexperienced, worked for Garrett; perhaps he did what he was told to do.

There exists still another version of the shooting. In *Alias Billy the Kid*, Sonnichsen provides the following account, taken from an April 15,

1944, interview with Jack Fountain, a son of the late Colonel Albert J. Fountain. Jack Fountain rode with Garrett for weeks at a time, and on one occasion the former sheriff of Lincoln County told him what he called "the straight of Billy's death." It took some time for Garrett to come to the point, but he finally said he would tell the true story. After Billy the Kid got away after killing Olinger and Bell, he explained, the county commissioners assigned him to bring in the young outlaw. Garrett learned that the Kid was in Fort Sumner. By the time Garrett and his deputies arrived at Maxwell's and tied their horses, the Kid was just in off the range and looking for something to eat. He was told Maxwell had just killed a steer. According to Fountain, Garrett said that beef was hanging in a little outer room from one of the vigas. "There was a candle and materials for making a light in the niche in the wall. He made a light and held it up while he cut. I was in Pete's room, talking. Billy heard something and asked Pete who was there. Pete said, 'Nobody.' I looked out at a perfect target—Billy lighting himself up with the candle. At first I was just going to wing him. Then I thought if he ever got to his gun it was him or me. My conscience bothers me about it now."

If Fountain's account is true, it explains the presence of a body outside of the room. Is Fountain credible? There is no reason to suspect he is any less credible than Pat Garrett.

Given the evidence available for determining what happened in Maxwell's room that night, there is little to support that Garrett was telling the truth about anything. Garrett and Upson's "recital of circumstances surrounding the Kid's death on the night of July 14, 1881," according to Nolan, "may have been the biggest lie of all."

The historical accounts of the shooting appear rife with inconsistencies and contradictions and, according to Nolan, "lies." Rather than clearing up the problem, they simply add to the confusion. How could so many people have so many different versions of what occurred that night, with most of them differing from Garrett's? None of the so-called facts relating to the death of Billy the Kid at the hands of Pat Garrett has ever been supported by logical and defensible evidence. By contrast, Roberts's account of what occurred that night makes as much sense as Garrett's and has never been proven wrong.

There is very little corroborative, logical evidence on which to base the claim that Billy the Kid was shot and killed by sheriff Pat Garrett on the night of July 14, 1881. The fact that Garrett contradicts himself and is contradicted by others many times about the event leaves numerous questions about what actually transpired that night.

There is more to ponder here. For a number of reasons, the best interest of Pat Garrett would have been to maintain that the man he shot and killed was Billy the Kid. If he were able to get away with it, he could avoid being charged with a serious mistake—killing an innocent man. If he could claim that the Kid died at his hands, he would obtain prestige for bringing an end to the Southwest's most famous outlaw, as well as a significant amount of reward money.

Desperate, Garrett may have presumed that the Kid, knowing that there was a price on his head and that he was destined to hang if caught, would leave the country for good. That is precisely what Roberts did.

Some have suggested there might have been a conspiracy. Could there have been collusion between Garrett and Poe to fabricate a story about the death of the armed and dangerous Billy the Kid? Given the fraternal allegiance between the two men, the possibility cannot be ruled out. Or, could Garrett and Poe sincerely have believed that the man killed that night was the Kid when he may have been Barlow? Poe had never seen the Kid, so he would have believed anything Garrett told him.

According to Roberts, he and Barlow once worked together on a ranch near Muleshoe, Texas. He doubted that Barlow was his real name, and he claimed that his friend was slightly younger, about the same size, and had dark hair and a beard. He was a heavy drinker and had been imbibing the night of July 14.

In 1948, an old man named Manuel Taylor related a Billy the Kid incident to L. S. Cardwell of Las Cruces, New Mexico. Taylor claimed that he knew Billy well during the time the two were in Silver City from 1868 to 1871. Taylor maintained that the man shot by Pat Garrett that night at Maxwell's was not Billy the Kid but a young cattle detective from somewhere in the east. Taylor also claimed that he ran into the Kid in Guadalajara, Mexico, in 1914, where they both recognized one another. According to Sonnichsen, Taylor was well known in his hometown of Hillsboro, New Mexico, and was reported to be "truthful and trustworthy."

And what of Deputy McKinney? If there were a plot to convince others that the Kid was shot and killed by Garrett, did McKinney go along with it? Tacitly, he did so by remaining quiet for a long time. McKinney, however, was not silent forever.

In a letter to William Waters, dated June 29, 1955, William V. Morrison provides some insight into McKinney's subsequent role in the events. In later years, according to a McKinney cousin, the lawman stated to relatives that he, McKinney, killed the man in Maxwell's bedroom "by mistake, and that the Kid got away."

In the same letter, Morrison also relates a portion of a telephone conversation he had with a grandson of McKinney. The grandson stated that the deputy "contended the man was killed on the outside and the Kid got away." This bit of information, if true, supports Roberts's version of the event and his mention of seeing a "body lying on the back porch."

Another incident related in the same letter dealt with a telephone call received by Ted Andress, the president of the law firm that Morrison represented at the time of the appeal for pardon. Andress states that the call came from a man who said that he was willing to testify that "McKinney had reminded Garrett in a saloon in Uvalde, Texas, that Garrett should know that he had not killed anyone that night."

The numerous accounts of the shooting in Maxwell's room on July 14, 1881, are not consistent, even the ones from those who were present and involved. Analysis of all of the accounts leads to the conclusion that Pat Garrett fabricated events and provided no credible evidence to indicate what actually occurred in Maxwell's bedroom that night or who was killed.

By contrast, the more scrutiny of the account provided by William Henry Roberts, the stronger his credibility.

EIGHT

---◆◆◆---

The Inquest

According to published history, Milnor Rudolph rode into Fort Sumner on the morning of July 15 and found the townspeople excited, confused, and angry. Garrett, Poe, and McKinney remained barricaded in Maxwell's bedroom, concerned they would be attacked by the angry mob of Billy the Kid sympathizers gathered outside of the house.

In *Billy the Kid: A Short and Violent Life*, Robert Utley writes that justice of the peace Alejandro Segura summoned Rudolph to assemble a coroner's jury and assume the role of foreman. Rudolph agreed, enlisted five men, and held a meeting in Maxwell's bedroom, where, according to Charles Frederick Rudulph, a descendant of Milnor's but who spells the name differently, the body still lay on the floor. In their books, Garrett and Poe both claimed the body had been taken to the carpenter shop for a wake shortly after the shooting. It is improbable that the body was reclaimed from the wake and repositioned on the floor.

Rudolph and the jurymen listened to Garrett and Maxwell recount the events of the previous evening. Rudolph then wrote out the report, and the jurors signed it or made their mark. They concluded that "William Bonney was killed by a shot in the left breast, in the region of the heart, fired from a pistol in the hand of Patrick F. Garrett, and our verdict is that the act of the said Garrett was justifiable homicide, and we are unanimous in the opinion that the gratitude of the whole community is due to the said Garrett for his act and that he deserves to be rewarded."

For reasons never completely explained, this coroner's jury report was never entered into the official records of San Miguel County. In fact, Justice Segura never even made an entry regarding the report in his own books. Even more perplexing and stunning is that the

Rudolph inquest was apparently the second coroner's report made that day!

Like the shooting, the inquest of the man Garrett claimed was Billy the Kid has also been shrouded in confusion and mystery. The speed with which the inquest was handled was peculiar and suspect. According to writer Frank Richard Prassell in *The Great American Outlaw*, "Lawmen of the era normally went to considerable effort to verify the deaths of fugitives for two good reasons: To foreclose a later charge of killing an innocent party and to facilitate the collection of rewards."

It is possible that Garrett knew he was guilty of killing an innocent man and therefore wanted the process to move quickly so that the victim could be buried before the mistake was discovered. It is also odd that the Rudolph report states that Garrett "deserves to be rewarded." Many believe the line, if not the entire report, was dictated by Garrett himself.

Another curious fact that bothers researchers of Western outlaw history is that Garrett did not have the body of one of the Southwest's, perhaps America's, most famous badmen placed on public display, a common practice during that time. Furthermore, Garrett did not take the time to pose for a photograph with the body, another common and accepted practice of the day. According to some versions of the incident, Garrett had the body locked in Maxwell's room overnight and allowed only a few to see it. Could Garrett, knowing the man he shot was not Billy the Kid, not have wanted the corpse placed on display or photographed because people would know it was not that of the Kid?

Even more bothersome is the fact that there were two coroner's reports, one made shortly after the shooting and the other, the Rudolph inquest, early the following morning. A. P. Anaya, a former member of the New Mexico state legislature, told George Fitzpatrick, editor of *New Mexico* magazine, that he and a friend "were called as members of the coroner's jury the night the Kid was killed, and that this jury wrote out a verdict stating simply that the Kid had come to his death as a result of a wound from a gun at the hands of Pat Garrett, officer." Whether the members of this jury actually saw the body of the slain man was never made clear.

Anaya claimed that this verdict was lost and that Garrett and Manuel Abreu wrote a second one, a "more flowery one for filing." New signatures other than Anaya's and those who witnessed the first report appeared on the second one. Anaya also stated that Milnor Rudolph was not a member of the original jury that viewed the body. The sequence of events relating to the two inquests is unusual, and the related contradictions and inconsistencies invite suspicion, particularly of the individual overseeing the proceedings—sheriff Pat Garrett. The origin of this report, a part of which was quoted earlier, likewise remains a mystery, and its authenticity has never been verified.

Why was a coroner's report never recorded in Lincoln County records? According to William A. Keleher, in *Violence in Lincoln County*, the second coroner's report was written in Spanish and attached to a cover letter written by Garrett. Keleher claims that a copy of the document was found during the 1930s in the Office of the Commissioner of Public Lands in the capitol building in Santa Fe, a claim that has never been substantiated. To date, no one has ever seen the document.

Curiously, in the copy of the verdict mentioned by Keleher, the words spoken by the man who entered Maxwell's bedroom were in English, "Who is it?" and not in Spanish, as stated by Garrett and Poe, thus providing even more inconsistency and contradiction. Additionally, some of the signers of the second report either misspelled their own names, or Rudolph misspelled them. Could it be that this report was a forgery, one arranged for and perhaps dictated by Pat Garrett himself? To further compound this growing confusion, E. B. Mann, in *Guns and Gunfighters*, wrote that only three witnesses identified the body and that one of them later stated that it was not Billy the Kid who was killed but another person. Whether anyone associated with the second coroner's report ever saw the body remains uncertain.

To this day, no one knows what happened to either of the two coroner's reports. Anaya stated that the first was lost, and Garrett claimed he filed the second with the district attorney of the First Judicial District in Las Vegas, the San Miguel County seat. Billy the Kid researcher Donald R. Lavash maintains that "the coroner's report is properly considered a death certificate and is on file at the NM-SRCA [New Mexico State Records Center and Archives] in Santa Fe." Why Lavash would make such a statement is unclear when no such document was ever located there and no one has ever been able to find it anywhere. On November 21, 1949, Alicia Romero, New Mexico's secretary of state, wrote to Morrison that there "is no record in this office of any coroner's verdict in the purported death of William H. Bonney."

According to an August 14, 1951, letter to Morrison from Fourth Judicial District attorney Jose E. Armijo, the coroner's report "is not now, and never has been, among the records in this office." That same month, however, the *El Paso Times* reported that writer and Lincoln County War historian Maurice G. Fulton claimed he had in his possession "a photostatic copy" of the coroner's report, though he never mentioned if it was the first or the second. Fulton discovered the report, he said, "while searching the file dealing with the reward for the killing of Billy the Kid . . . among the records of the office of the Secretary of the Territory of New Mexico." The document was immediately challenged and, to date, has never been verified as authentic.

In other words, the death of Billy the Kid was never officially recorded in the state of New Mexico. There is, in fact, no legal proof of the death of Billy the Kid.

Pat Garrett never collected the five-hundred-dollar reward offered by New Mexico governor Lew Wallace for the apprehension of Billy the Kid. Garrett petitioned for the reward money on July 20, 1881. The reward was denied by acting governor W. G. Ritch. According to writer Jon Tuska, some questions were raised relative to whether Garrett had really killed Billy the Kid. A few researchers claim that Garrett's request for the reward was denied because his application was not in proper legal form. Others refer to the problem generated by the purported death certificate, which was never found. Author Tuska suggests that after Garrett was turned down, Charlie Green, the editor of the *Santa Fe New Mexican* and a Garrett crony, recommended to the sheriff that he have a new coroner's report, a third one, drawn up. The document was written, according to Tuska, by Pete Maxwell's brother-in-law Manuel Abreu, and it contained signatures of men "who had not been present at the original hearing and it contains obviously slanted statements which indicate for what use it was intended."

Clearly, Garrett was not beyond being duplicitous and self-serving at the expense of truth. If Garrett had killed the right man in Maxwell's bedroom, none of these ploys would be necessary. To cover up his mistake of killing the wrong man, Garrett hurried along not one but two inquests, refused to place the body on display, refused to have his photograph made with the corpse, had the body buried posthaste, then almost a week later initiated a third coroner's report! And for what reason? There can be only one logical explanation—the dead man was not Billy the Kid.

Tuska states that it is "quite possible that the original document mentioned that the Kid was unarmed and was therefore suppressed." Tuska also raises the question of whether the coroner's jury, made up of men largely sympathetic to the Kid, would have concluded by recommending the reward not be paid to Garrett. Perhaps that is the reason why the original became "lost." Since Garrett was the official in charge, he bears responsibility for losing it and orchestrating the second report, the one that was more favorable to him.

In spite of Garrett's difficulties in collecting the reward, crony James J. Dolan raised $1,150 and presented it to the sheriff. According to an article in the *Las Vegas Optic*, rancher John Chisum gave the sheriff another $1,000. An article appearing in an August 5, 1951, *El Paso Times* stated that a total of an additional $2,300 was collected for Garrett from citizens in Santa Fe, Las Vegas, Silver City, Las Cruces, and Mesilla.

Finally, on February 18, 1882, after Garrett bought approximately five hundred dollars' worth of drinks for members of the New Mexico territorial legislature, they voted to pass an act providing the reward money for "the arrest of Billy the Kid." According to Sonnichsen, the legislature at the time was "heavily loaded" with Garrett's henchmen. Apparently none of the New Mexico legislators was aware, or cared, that Garrett never arrested anyone and that the identity of the man he killed was in dispute even then. This act, written by the legislators, credits Garrett with killing Billy the Kid "on or about the month of August, 1881."

Given the facts related to the events following the shooting of the man in Maxwell's bedroom and the various inquests, concluding without a doubt that the dead man was Billy the Kid seems questionable. Given the intense efforts by Garrett and others to circumvent the truth, the likelihood is great that all involved knew it was not Billy the Kid who had been killed.

NINE

❖❖❖

The Burial

The body of the man allegedly killed by Garrett was prepared and dressed for burial immediately following the second inquest. On the afternoon of July 15, the dead man was interred in a wooden coffin at the Fort Sumner military cemetery next to the graves of Tom O'Folliard and Charlie Bowdre, friends of Billy the Kid.

On July 28, an obituary appeared in the *Grant County Herald*, a Silver City newspaper. Titled "Exit 'The Kid'" and written by editor S. M. Ashenfelter, the article stated, in part, "Since his escape from the Lincoln County jail," the outlaw Billy the Kid "has allowed his beard to grow, and he has stained his skin brown to look like a Mexican."

Like the shooting and the inquests, the burial of the man Pat Garrett claimed was Billy the Kid has not escaped criticism and controversy. The interment proceeded at an astonishingly rapid pace; Garrett, apparently, could not get the body in the ground fast enough.

Before being transported to the Fort Sumner cemetery, the body of the dead man was dressed and placed in a hastily constructed wooden casket. Though difficult to verify, there is a possibility that only two or three people other than Garrett, Poe, and McKinney ever saw the body of the dead man on the floor of Maxwell's bedroom.

Leon Metz, in *Pat Garrett: The Story of a Western Lawman*, brings up the possibility that passing off any body as that of Billy the Kid could easily have been done "since neither John Poe nor Tip McKinney recognized the Kid, and both would be inclined to accept almost any body that Garrett claimed was Billy's." Garrett could then petition for the reward, says Metz, as well as the honor and prestige that went with killing the Southwest's most noted outlaw.

Ashenfelter claimed that the Kid disguised himself by staining "his skin brown to look like a Mexican." The description of the body fits not that of Billy the Kid but rather Billy Barlow, the man William Henry Roberts insisted was killed. In *Alias Billy the Kid*, Sonnichsen and Morrison relate some secondhand information about a man named Arthur Hyde. During a 1914 interview, Hyde stated that it was a young Mexican who was shot, one who looked a lot like Billy the Kid, and that he was set up by Pat Garrett.

Only six-and-a-half months before the shooting in Fort Sumner, J. H. Koogler, editor of the *Las Vegas Gazette*, interviewed the Kid while he was in town awaiting transportation to Mesilla for trial. In describing the outlaw, Koogler wrote, "There was nothing very mannish about him in appearance, for he looked and acted a mere boy. He is about five feet eight or nine inches tall, slightly built and lithe, weighing about 140; a frank open countenance, looking like a school boy, with the traditional silky fuzz on his upper lip; clear blue eyes, with a roguish snap about them; light hair and complexion."

The body of the dead man that was placed in the casket was described by newspaperman Ashenfelter as having dark skin and a beard. The Kid was never known to have dark skin or dark hair, and given that his facial hair was described as "silky fuzz," any beard he might have grown would have been insignificant.

According to Dr. J. M. Tanner in *Growth at Adolescence*, sexual maturity ratings (SMRs) are developmental stages not necessarily related to chronological age. SMRs 1 and 2 are associated with early adolescence in males ten to fifteen years of age. During SMR 2 in males, facial hair may appear, and it is often of a fine and silky texture. Middle adolescence (SMRs 3 and 4) typically begins between years twelve and fifteen. Late adolescence (SMR 5) is generally reached between the fourteenth and sixteenth years, although may not appear until much later.

During SMR 5, which according to Tanner can occur "as late as the early twenties in some individuals," secondary sex characteristics begin to develop. In the male, facial hair spreads to the chin and chest. Tanner points out that the length of time between SMR 2, associated with silky fuzz, and SMR 5, associated with a beard, can be as long as three years.

If Billy the Kid, at age twenty to twenty-one, was still exhibiting "silky fuzz on his upper lip" as described by Koogler, this indicates he was experiencing delayed sexual maturity. Based on Tanner's research, it is improbable to impossible that, given the chronology of the SMR sequences, the Kid could have gone from silky fuzz to dark skin and a beard in only six-and-a-half months.

Based on the descriptions provided by Ashenfelter and Koogler, the body in the casket could not have been that of Billy the Kid. The biological processes associated with such dramatic endochronological changes do not exist such that they would cause a light-complected lad with silky fuzz to evolve to a dark-skinned man with a beard in such a short time.

In a March 1980 article that appeared in *Frontier Times* magazine, writer Ben W. Kemp shares some pertinent information told to him by his uncle John Graham, who was a Fort Sumner resident and who knew Billy the Kid. On the morning following the shooting, Graham and a Mexican were sent to dig the grave for Garrett's victim. Graham stated that when the wagon carrying the casket arrived, it was accompanied by an armed guard "with strict orders to see that no one opened it to see what was inside." The word used was *what*, not *who*.

According to Kemp, Graham agreed with John Poe that the body of the dead man was removed from Maxwell's bedroom a short time after the shooting and not the following morning, as stated by others. Kemp quotes Graham, however, as saying that an acquaintance told him that the man killed by Garrett was one of Maxwell's hired hands.

The late Verna Reed, a Carlsbad, New Mexico, resident, said that her great-grandfather Joseph Wood helped with the burial. All of his life, Wood insisted that the coffin contained a side of beef, the one that hung near Maxwell's room.

So, who was buried on July 15, 1881? There is not a scintilla of verifiable evidence that it was the man known as the outlaw Billy the Kid. There is more compelling evidence that suggests the body was that of Billy Barlow, thus corroborating William Henry Roberts's version of the events.

The original wooden marker placed at the head of the grave of the man killed by Garrett was often used by drunks for target practice and eventually reduced to splinters. Shortly after, according to a 1938 interview with Carolatta Baca published in *They Knew Billy the Kid*, very few people in Fort Sumner knew the location of the original gravesite. Twenty-two of the bodies in the cemetery were those of soldiers, many of them lacking identification. In 1906, they were disinterred and reburied in the Santa Fe National Cemetery. Supporting evidence is lacking that the remains of the man Garrett wanted the world to believe was Billy the Kid were among them.

On a number of occasions during the past 120 years, the nearby Pecos River has flooded, inflicting damage to the cemetery located near the adjacent floodplain. High-velocity floodwaters were observed and recorded carrying away headstones and markers with coffins and their contents. By the 1930s, as a result of flood damage, there was little left of the cemetery that was recognizable.

In 1937, the four pallbearers who carried the casket containing the remains of the man shot by Garrett were still alive and living in Fort Sumner. Vicente Otero, Yginio Salazar, Jesus Silva, and Charlie Foor were assembled at the old cemetery and asked to agree on the original location. They were unable to do so, each man selecting a different site. Finally, they agreed to compromise by placing a marker in the approximate center of the four different choices. According to George E. Kaiser, a resident of Artesia, New Mexico, there was another major flood in 1943, which washed away the newer marker as well as a few other graves.

The current gravesite of the man Garrett identified as Billy the Kid, as well as those of Tom O'Folliard and Charlie Bowdre, is an important tourist attraction for the town of Fort Sumner. There is no proof that Billy the Kid is buried under the marker.

Billy the Kid. (A. and S. Upham collection.)

William Henry Roberts, alias Billy the Kid, in his late fifties. (Author collection.)

Pat Garrett. (Western History Collections, University of Oklahoma Library.)

Ash Upson, friend of sheriff Pat Garrett and principal author of The Authentic Life of Billy the Kid. *(Special Collections, University of Arizona Library, Papers of Walter Noble Burns.)*

John Henry Tunstall, friend and employer of Billy the Kid. (Special Collections, University of Arizona Library, Papers of Walter Noble Burns.)

Alexander McSween. (Special Collections, University of Arizona Library, Papers of Walter Noble Burns.)

William Henry Roberts and William V. Morrison. (Author collection.)

William Henry Roberts and wife, Melinda, 1950. (Author collection.)

Location of Buffalo Gap, Texas.

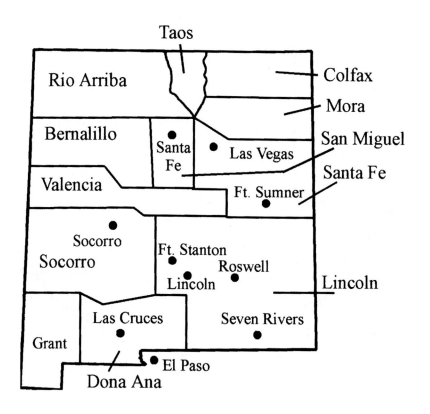

New Mexico Territory, 1880, with principal cities frequented by Billy the Kid.

William Brady, sheriff of Lincoln County. (Special Collections, University of Arizona Library, Papers of Walter Noble Burns.)

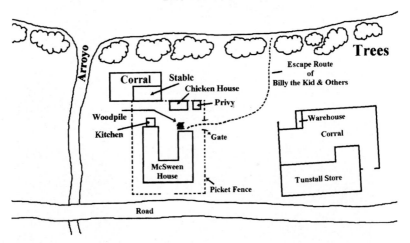

McSween house and yard and escape route of Billy the Kid and companions during the Lincoln County War.

United States deputy marshal Robert Olinger. (Nita Stewart Haley Memorial Library.)

Godfrey Gauss, who cut Billy the Kid's leg irons during the outlaw's escape from the Lincoln County Courthouse. (Nita Stewart Haley Memorial Library.)

Purported photograph of William Henry Roberts at approximately thirty years of age. (Author collection.)

William Henry Roberts and New Mexico governor Thomas J. Mabry, 1950. (Author collection.)

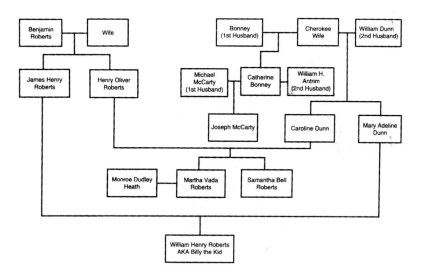

Genealogy of William Henry Roberts (Billy the Kid) reconstructed from the Roberts family Bible and the family Bible of the late Martha Vada Roberts, a distant cousin.

William Henry Roberts as a detective for the Anti-Horsethief Association. (Author collection.)

Both sides of the Spanish Civil War medal presented to members of Teddy Roosevelt's Rough Riders who participated in the Cuba campaign; this one was found among Roberts's belongings. (Author collection.)

Deputy John W. Poe. (Zimmerman Library, University of New Mexico.)

The Maxwell house. Pete Maxwell's bedroom, where sheriff Pat Garrett shot the man he thought was Billy the Kid, is located in the near corner. (Nita Stewart Haley Memorial Library.)

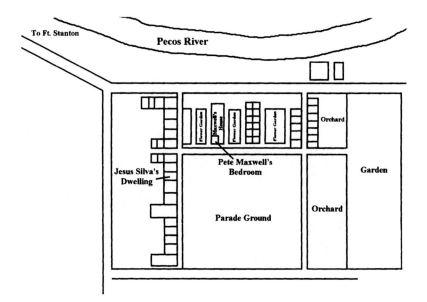

Fort Sumner, 1881.

Lincoln County Courthouse, 1884. (Nita Stewart Haley Memorial Library.)

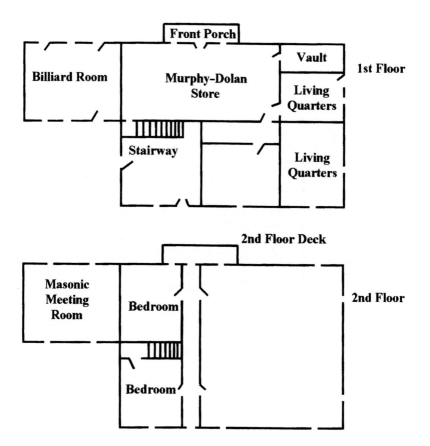

Floor plan of the Murphy Building during the time it served as the Murphy–Dolan Store.

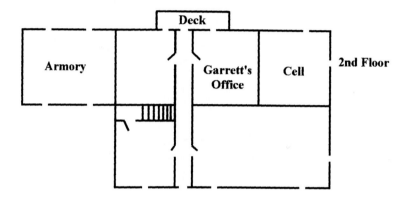

Floor plan of the second floor of the Murphy Building during the time it served as the Lincoln County Courthouse, 1881.

Yginio Salazar. (Special Collections, University of Arizona Library, Papers of Walter Noble Burns.)

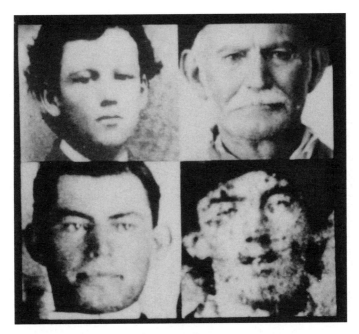

Four images used in the University of Texas photo-comparison study. Clockwise from upper left: a purported photo of a young Billy the Kid; William Henry Roberts at age ninety; Billy the Kid; a purported photograph of Roberts as a young man. (Author collection.)

Deluvina Maxwell as an elderly woman. (Zimmerman Library, University of New Mexico.)

William Henry Roberts, alias Billy the Kid, and William V. Morrison. (Author collection.)

Purported photograph of Catherine Bonney, Billy the Kid's aunt. (Author collection.)

William Henry Roberts, alias Billy the Kid, at ninety years of age. (Author collection.)

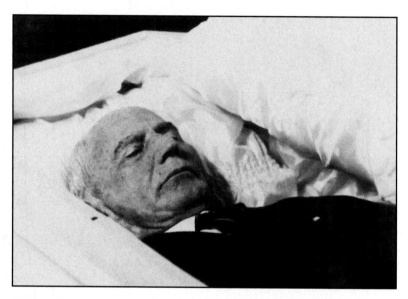

William Henry Roberts, alias Billy the Kid, in death. (Author collection.)

TEN

◆◆◆

Tracking William Henry Roberts

An examination of post–Fort Sumner elements of William Henry Roberts's life yields a number of events with potential for research and investigation with the objective of verifying or renouncing his claims. For example, Roberts stated that he worked for the Anti-Horsethief Association on three occasions between 1885 through 1889. Roberts also claimed that he rode with the Buffalo Bill Cody Wild West Show, a well-known touring Western circus that was popular during the latter part of the nineteenth century and the early part of the twentieth century. In 1898 he enlisted in Teddy Roosevelt's Rough Riders and was sent to Cuba. In 1902, Roberts stated that he operated his own Wild West show for a short time.

ANTI-HORSETHIEF ASSOCIATION

William Henry Roberts claimed that he worked for an organization called the Anti-Horsethief Association. Some who have insisted that Roberts was a fraud have maintained there was no such thing as an Anti-Horsethief Association and that he made it up. In a letter to Frederic Bean, Donald Cline states, "No Anti-Horsethief Association ever existed according to Oklahoma and Texas State archives and records or cattlemen's association."

On February 9, 1983, Teresa O'Guin Capps, an employee of the University of Oklahoma Western Collections Library, verified the existence of the Anti-Horsethief Association in a letter and that the "association had chapters in different areas," chapters which were scattered.

In an August 25, 1951, letter to Ola Everhard of Texas, a man named Ozark Jack Berlin, living in Veedersburg, Indiana, mentioned William Henry Roberts's link with the Anti-Horsethief Association. In the letter, Berlin recalls that Roberts, "if I remember rite was a Horse

thief Detective. I was with him one nite at a dance at the Round Top
Mountain in the Creek Nation where there was some shooting dun. I
was shot thru and left for Dead. He lade down on the floor and feened
death until the shooting was over."

A few days following the death of Roberts, in Hico 1950, an Anti-
Horsethief Association badge, a small image of a horse's head made of
bone with a yellow gold-wire bridle, was found among his possessions
and its authenticity verified by Capps. Before he died, Roberts produced an old photograph for Morrison that showed him as a younger
man sitting astride a horse that was branded with a *C*, the brand, according to librarian Capps, of the Anti-Horsethief Association. A similar photograph was found in 1988 in a trunk containing Roberts's
few possessions, provided by his stepgrandson Bill Allison.

In spite of the assertions of Cline and others, the Anti-Horsethief
Association is a matter of historical record, and based on the evidence, Roberts was employed by it.

BUFFALO BILL'S WILD WEST SHOW

While attempting to find a link between Roberts and Buffalo Bill's
Wild West Show, R. I. Frost, curator of the Buffalo Bill Museum in
Cody, Wyoming, found that "few records of Buffalo Bill's Wild West
Show exist." According to Frost, when the show closed in Denver,
Colorado, in August 1913, "all records were destroyed by burning."

Frost further explained that the Wild West Show "operated five
summer months, May through September, each year employing about
600 people." There was a great deal of turnover of employees from
year to year, and employee lists by year "were not published except in
a few isolated cases."

In spite of the fact that records of show employees were either nonexistent, lost, or burned, evidence for Roberts's association with
Buffalo Bill's Wild West Show was provided in the form of a signed
and notarized affidavit from one Robert E. Lee.

Lee, who worked as a bodyguard for Cody, knew that Roberts was
Billy the Kid and affirmed that he "was riding in Buffalo Bill's Wild
West Show in Chicago, Illinois, in 1883; that the Kid was one of the
best riders in the show." Another affidavit, by Dewitt Travis, also
states that Roberts "rode in the Wild West Shows of Buffalo Bill and
Pawnee Bill."

In an August 1929 issue of the *Texas Monthly*, a cowhand named
Cyclone Denton was quoted as saying he once worked on the old Gila

Ranch in Arizona with Billy the Kid and that the two of them later rode for Buffalo Bill.

Rough Riders

With regard to Roberts's claim that he served as a member of Roosevelt's Rough Riders, research failed to find his name on any enlistment rosters. Since Roberts had a history of using aliases, he may have gone undetected.

Two days after Roberts's funeral, evidence was discovered that served to lend support to his Rough Riders claim. While going through items in an old trunk belonging to Roberts, his widow, Melinda, and her grandson Bill Allison discovered a medal they had never seen before. General Henry Blake of the New Mexico Military Institute in Roswell, New Mexico, identified the medal, verified its authenticity, and consulted a reference book on its official use. The commemoration was a Spanish War Service Medal, sometimes called the National Guard Medal. Designed by Colonel J. R. M. Taylor, U.S. Army, the face of the medal displays a sheathed Roman sword lying on a tablet inscribed "For Service in the Spanish War." The medal was authorized in 1918 for persons who served between April 20, 1898, and April 11, 1899.

This medal was given to veterans of the Cuban campaign.

Roberts's Wild West Show

After returning from Cuba, William Henry Roberts claimed that he started his own Wild West Show, which he operated off and on until 1904. No records can be found relating specifically to Roberts's business. Several Wild West shows were traveling and performing throughout the United States and Canada during that time, but the records for most of them are nonexistent. The only reference to Roberts's show that has been found was in the affadavit by Dewitt Travis, who stated that Roberts, after performing with Buffalo Bill and Pawnee Bill, later started a "Wild West show of his own."

Due to the passage of time—in some cases over a century—locating substantive information pertinent to other claims advanced by Roberts proved difficult. In the case of his claim that he resided for a time in Sonora with the Yaqui Indians, records for such things do not exist. In 1951, however, an acquaintance of Roberts, Dewitt Travis, stated in a signed and notarized affidavit that the Kid "ranched in

Old Mexico," returned to Texas about 1884, and "took the name the Texas Kid." In other cases, as a result of the passage of so much time, documents that may have supported a claim have been destroyed, lost, or removed.

Further compounding the difficulties in tracking and validating Roberts's past was his lifelong habit of using aliases. Roberts told Morrison he used more than a dozen aliases and confessed his real name only a short time before he died. As Billy the Kid, Roberts was doing his best to keep a low profile and remain as anonymous as possible because he was convinced he was still under sentence to be hanged. For most of his adult life, Roberts used the name of a cousin, Oliver L. Roberts, who was born in 1867, ran away from home in 1884, and died alone in Indian Territory several years later.

Part of the difficulty in researching Roberts's claims was related to the information he provided Morrison. In several cases, Roberts could not remember most of the aliases he used during his lifetime. In other cases, Morrison simply did not probe deep enough during the interviews. Author C. L. Sonnichsen intended to interview Roberts in depth, relative to his life as Billy the Kid and beyond, but the old man's death following the meeting with Governor Thomas Mabry prevented Sonnichsen from doing so.

ELEVEN

◆◆◆

Evidence

Evidence is, in and of itself, not proof. Evidence can lead to proof, and proof can sometimes be determined by the available evidence. Evidence can be soft or hard, but to yield proof, it must be cogent and acceptable, it must be reasonable, and it must be valid. There is abundant evidence that the man killed by Pat Garrett in 1881 was not Billy the Kid. At the same time, there is a significant body of evidence that advances the notion that William Henry Roberts could be the famous outlaw. To some, the evidence is logical, compelling, and defensible. To others, it remains subjective and open to interpretation.

PHYSICAL SIMILARITIES

William Henry Roberts had the size, shape, and general overall appearance of the outlaw Billy the Kid. Roberts has been described as slim, spry, and muscular. In *Alias Billy the Kid*, Sonnichsen writes that at ninety years of age Roberts was in excellent physical condition and stood "straight as an arrow . . . about five feet, eight inches tall" in cowboy boots.

One of Billy the Kid's most characteristic features was his two protruding front teeth, "especially visible when he smiled or laughed, which was nearly always," writes Robert Utley. According to Dewitt Travis in an affadavit of identification, Roberts possessed such teeth until they were removed by a Gladewater, Texas, dentist in 1931. Following Roberts's death, relatives going through a trunk containing his belongings found the two large front incisors.

Another significant feature was the Kid's prominent ears. A comparison of the only authenticated photograph of Billy the Kid with frontal images of William Henry Roberts reveals a remarkable similarity in the size and shape of the ears. Roberts, like the Kid, had a left ear that protruded farther than the right.

Billy the Kid had relatively large wrists and disproportionately small hands and was able to fold them in such a way that they were made narrower than his wrists, thus enabling him to pull free from handcuffs. According to Sonnichsen, Roberts also possessed "small, neat hands with well-shaped fingers, unusually large wrists, heavy forearms, and well developed biceps." Once, when requested by Morrison, Roberts laid his thumbs inside his palms, held out his hands, and showed how his larger wrists merged into small hands without a bulge.

Billy the Kid's eyes were described as being bluish grey and dotted with tiny specks of brown. According to Sonnichsen and Morrison, Roberts had the same kind of eyes. A number of people who had known Billy the Kid during the time of the Lincoln County War and who were introduced to Roberts maintained that the eyes of the old man possessed the same characteristics as those of the outlaw.

When Billy the Kid ran into the main street of Lincoln to retrieve a pistol from the body of the fallen Sheriff Brady, he was shot in the right hip by Deputy Hindman. Roberts displayed a bullet wound scar in the same location. At least two people who had known Billy the Kid stated that Roberts walked like him, talked like him, and even laughed exactly like him. Some seventy years following the alleged death of Billy the Kid, William Henry Roberts manifested virtually every physical characteristic of the famous outlaw.

ROBERTS'S REVELATIONS

When William Henry Roberts was being interviewed by Morrison in 1949, he related a number of events, experiences, and features pertinent to the Lincoln County physical and cultural landscape, to noted and obscure personalities, and to the Lincoln County War that were generally unknown to most people. The information was so esoteric that only a few dedicated researchers were even aware of it. Much of it had never appeared in print but was found in letters and records tucked away in little-known archival collections scattered throughout the country.

Roberts was described by Morrison as semiliterate. Examples of his handwriting show that it was a barely legible scrawl, and when correspondence was necessary, it was almost always written by his wife, Melinda. In addition, claimed Morrison, Roberts could barely read. Roberts was not capable of researching pertinent or even minor aspects of the Lincoln County War, many of which were stored in obscure archives, and he would not have known what he was reading in the unlikely event he would have ever encountered specific documents. Roberts contributed a number of observations, several concerning obscure and unrecorded events, that ultimately proved to be accurate.

Floor Plan of the Lincoln County Courthouse

When William Henry Roberts entered the old Murphy–Dolan Store turned Lincoln County Courthouse in the company of Morrison in 1949, he appeared nervous and disoriented. He informed Morrison that the inside stairway was the same as it was in 1881 but that the two outside stairways on the front of the building leading to the second-floor deck had been added.

Roberts also told Morrison that the inside stairway started on the first floor on the west side of the building and ran toward the east and into a large hall on the second floor, which was oriented north-south. On the east side of the hall, he said, was Garrett's office. From there, another door opened into the room where the convicted outlaw was chained. Across the hall from Garrett's office, said Roberts, was the armory. During his visit, none of what he remembered about the courthouse was what was found on this part of the second floor, which today is open space with no walls or offices.

In the R. N. Mullin Collection, housed at the J. Evatts Haley History Center in Midland, Texas, an 1884 photograph of the Lincoln County Courthouse taken from across the street and several yards to the northeast of the building shows only a single outside stairway leading from the second-floor deck to the ground. The stairway appears to have been constructed sometime after the deck, as it is of a different style and color.

According to J. W. Hendron, in a 1939 article about the courthouse, in 1878 "there were no steps" leading to the deck on the second floor, and "there was no roof over it." In April 1881, when Billy the Kid escaped from the courthouse, there were no stairs on the outside of the building. Hendron says that no one is certain how the Kid left the courthouse. "Some say he came down one of the pillars supporting the balcony and others say he left by the back stairs."

Hendron says that the stairs to the second floor, or balcony, were constructed in 1884, and at the time they consisted of "a narrow staircase from the east end of the balcony." Several years later, presumably in the 1890s, "two full-width staircases were built on both sides of the balcony in front and a roof was built over Major Murphy's sun porch." By 1910, "an old-timer who had not seen the Murphy–Dolan store since the days of the Lincoln County War would not have recognized it."

Hendron also provided an early floor plan of the building with a description of the interior, both of which coincided precisely with Roberts's recollections. Roberts's descriptions of the interior and exterior architecture of the building as it existed in 1881 were complete and exact. He would not have known such long-forgotten and esoteric detail had he not been there.

Colonel Dudley's Black Troopers

Roberts told Morrison that, following the killing of Tunstall, he and several of the Regulators escorted Alexander McSween to his house in the town of Lincoln. After fighting off the sheriff's posse, most of the Regulators took refuge in the McSween house while the remainder sought cover at Tunstall's store, immediately to the east. The Murphy men began shooting at the house, and the fighting continued throughout the day. The next morning, according to Roberts's taped recollection, "Colonel Dudley rode into town with those nigger soldiers" and demanded that McSween stop the fighting.

The Regulators explained to Dudley that they had not started the fighting and that they were only protecting themselves. Later, Roberts claimed that Dudley stationed some of his black troopers on the side of the hill south of the main road, where they commenced firing on the house.

Before Roberts's revelation about the black soldiers, few researchers steeped in Billy the Kid and Lincoln County War history were aware of the racial makeup of Dudley's charges or their exact role in the skirmish. For years, historians disputed the contention that the troopers fired on the McSween house. Research by Sonnishcsen into the nature of the soldiers stationed at nearby Fort Stanton in 1881 eventually revealed that the infantrymen were predominantly black.

Roberts stated that Dudley, accompanied by black soldiers, "rode into town." This is verified by a statement by Martin Chavez, a participant in the Lincoln County War, who told Miguel Antonio Otero during an interview in the 1930s that "Colonel Dudley had arrived with a mounted company of negro troops." Historical documents, as well as the court record of Dudley's subsequent court martial, unmistakably show that the colonel, accompanied by four officers, entered the town of Lincoln on horseback and, as described by Utley in *Billy the Kid: A Short and Violent Life*, were "followed by eleven mounted troopers of the black Ninth Cavalry and twenty-four white footmen of the Fifteenth Infantry."

In 1949, Roberts could not have known any of this obscure history had he not been present while it was taking place.

McSween House and Yard

Between July 14 and 19, 1878, the McSween house was under siege by Lincoln County law enforcement personnel and the U.S. Army. On the evening of July 19, the house was set afire. According to some Billy the Kid historians, the Kid assumed the mantle of command at this point and proposed that he and a few others attempt a break from the burning structure and try to reach the safety of the nearby Tunstall store. During the flight, Harvey Morris, who was studying law with McSween, was killed, and the heavy fire from the opposing force drove the rest north, toward the safety of the river.

William Henry Roberts recalled the escape from the McSween house during a taped interview with Morrison: "By dark, the house had burned except for the kitchen which was nearly gone. About dusk . . . we decided to make a run for it. The women had already left the house, the building was caving in from the fire."

Roberts precisely recalled a window at the east side of the kitchen, and he also remembered that a door opened at the northeast corner into an area between the house and an adobe wall. "There was a board fence running between the house and the corral, running north and south," said Roberts, "with a gate at the northeast corner of the yard." Just east of the fence and on the other side of the corral was Tunstall's store building. Several Murphy men were stationed just across the Rio Penasco, which flowed just to the house. "The gate in the board fence opened toward the Tunstall store," recalled Roberts.

Someone opened the back door of the kitchen and peered out to see Murphy employee Bob Beckwith and several soldiers attempting to rush the house. Harvey Morris, who was studying law with McSween, was the first to step out of the kitchen door. Roberts was next, followed by Jose Chavez, McSween, Romero, and Zamora. Roberts remembered spotting Beckwith standing near the adobe wall and that he fired at him. "I think one of my bullets killed him when I made a run for it." An instant later, "Morris was shot down in front of me. I ran through the gate with both .44s blazing, and Jose Chavez was right behind me. He and I ran toward Tunstall's store. We got fired at, and then we turned toward the river. A bullet went through my hat as

I came out the gate. I lost my hat and one six-shooter crossing the river. There was brush and undergrowth to hide us along the river."

By the time they reached the gate, McSween and Zamora were driven back by a fusillade from Murphy's men and the soldiers. They ran toward a small enclosure between the house and the adobe wall. Roberts described how "McSween and the others started for the gate a second time, but were driven back where they were killed by Jones and Kinney and those soldiers of Dudley's. O'Folliard, Salazar, and the rest of the boys started through. All of them escaped except Salazar who was cut down beside the door. They thought he was dead, but Salazar crawled out that night after everyone left. He told me how McSween and the rest got killed."

The McSween house burned to the ground that evening and was never rebuilt. Today in Lincoln there is only a patch of grass-covered ground where the house once stood, and a historical marker is the only indication that it ever existed.

Seven decades after the shoot-out at the McSween residence, William Henry Roberts was able to recall numerous precise details relative to the layout of the yard, fences, walls, gates, the house in general, and the surroundings in particular, even seemingly unimportant features of the backyard, such as the enclosure where the firewood was kept and the direction the gate swung open.

Roberts could not have read about such things and could not have discussed such detailed minutiae with old-timers from the area—his knowledge could have come only from personal experience.

Federal and Territorial Indictments

In 1949, only a few researchers were aware that, during the trial of Billy the Kid at Mesilla during March and April 1881, the federal charge for killing Buckshot Roberts was dismissed and that the Kid was represented by Ira Leonard. Two days later, the Kid, this time represented by John D. Bail and Albert J. Fountain, was charged by the territory of New Mexico for the killing of Sheriff Brady, for which the outlaw was sentenced to hang. Since this information was virtually unknown before Roberts's revelation, most devoted readers of Billy the Kid history are unaware of these fine and obscure points.

During an interview with Morrison, Roberts stated, "In April I pleaded to the federal indictment, and it was thrown out of court. Judge Leonard represented me on this indictment. He got it thrown out by the judge. Then I was put on trial for the murder of Sheriff

Brady, a territorial charge. Judge Fountain was appointed to represent me on the territorial charge."

Once again, Roberts demonstrated an impressive intimacy with a relatively minor and obscure aspect of the life of Billy the Kid. Only a person who had spent time examining specific court records would have known about it—or someone who was there.

Escape from Jail

In *The Authentic Life of Billy the Kid*, Pat Garrett writes that Billy the Kid initiated his escape from the Lincoln County jail by breaking into the armory, seizing a pistol, and shooting and killing one of his guards, deputy J. W. Bell.

In Billy the Kid history, the only consistency is inconsistency or contradiction. A second version of the escape has the Kid finding a pistol wrapped in newspaper and hidden in the privy. The gun was allegedly placed there by a friend, Sam Corbett. Following his visit to the privy and after reaching the head of the stairs leading toward his second-floor confinement, the Kid supposedly pulled the gun and shot Bell.

In *Lincoln County War*, author Maurice G. Fulton refers to the latter account as "the official one," although how he came to this conclusion has never been explained. The former, and conflicting, account is the one touted by the New Mexico Monument Association, according to a sign in the Lincoln County Courthouse Museum. How this determination was made is likewise a mystery.

While being interviewed by Morrison in 1949, during the time they were visiting the second-floor confinement area in the Lincoln County courthouse, William Henry Roberts provided yet a third version of the escape. Olinger had gone to lunch, and Deputy Bell and Roberts were alone. Roberts was sitting on a wooden box, handcuffed, shackled, and chained to the floor. Bell was sitting by a window reading a paper when Roberts asked to be unlocked and taken to the outhouse behind the courthouse. At first Bell objected, not wanting to take a chance unlocking the prisoner without another guard nearby. Finally, he went into Sheriff Garrett's office and obtained the key that unlocked the heavy padlock. Roberts said, "At this moment I slipped my right hand from the cuff and, holding them by the left, I hit him in the back of the head. He tumbled over on the floor. When he came up, he was looking down the barrel of his own six-shooter."

Roberts assured Bell he would not be hurt if he would do as he was told. He ordered the deputy to walk through the office and unlock the armory door. Roberts wanted to lock the deputy inside while he made his escape. Silently, Bell walked through the office, but as he stepped into the hall, he made a break for the stairway. "With the fourteen-inch chain between my leg irons, I couldn't run," said Roberts, "so I jumped and slid across the floor to the left toward the stairs." On reaching the head of the stairs, Roberts aimed and fired at Bell below. "I pulled the trigger, and the bullet struck the wall on that side. It must have ricocheted and struck him under the arm, coming out the other side. Bell fell down the steps, dying as he fell."

Roberts's version differed significantly from the two "official" accounts. There was, of course, only one surviving witness to this event, only one person who knew the truth of what had occurred, and that was Billy the Kid himself.

Five days after the escape, a letter in the Santa Fe *New Mexican* stated that "Bell lay dead in the backyard with one bullet through him and two gashes on his head, apparently cut by a blow from the handcuffs." This recorded observation renders Roberts's account a high degree of plausibility.

Many years later, the Kid's good friend John Meadows told Maurice G. Fulton that shortly after the escape, the outlaw explained to him how it was accomplished. The Kid, according to Meadows, slipped the cuff off one wrist and swung the loose end in vicious blows that opened two gashes in Bell's scalp. Observers noted that as Billy the Kid made his escape from the courthouse he was not wearing handcuffs.

Letter to Governor Wallace

With regard to the shootout at the Greathouse Ranch, most Billy the Kid historians have written that the Kid killed a man named Jimmy Carlyle, a White Oaks resident and deputy who entered the house to encourage or intimidate the Kid into surrendering. According to many accounts, Carlyle was killed by the Kid as he jumped through a window while attempting to escape.

During one of his taped interviews with Morrison, William Henry Roberts recalled that, following the shootout at the Greathouse Ranch, he fled to Las Vegas, New Mexico, where he learned from an article in the *Las Vegas Gazette* that Billy the Kid was responsible for the killing of James Carlyle. Roberts told Morrison he immediately had a letter written to Governor Lew Wallace, dated December 12, 1880, explaining the events of the confrontation and that Carlyle was killed by members of his own posse and maintaining he was innocent of the charge.

When Roberts was interviewed in 1949, very few people were aware of the existence of this letter, which is part of a collection housed at the William Henry Smith Memorial Library in Indianapolis, Indiana.

Roberts could not have knowledge of such a document unless he was responsible for having it written.

Jim East

After surrendering to Garrett's posse at Stinking Springs on December 23, 1880, Roberts told Morrison that he was taken by wagon to Fort Sumner. He claimed that the following day Pete Maxwell's wife sent an Indian servant girl to ask Garrett to allow the Kid to visit with them before being transported to Santa Fe. Roberts recalled that he was chained to outlaw Dave Rudabaugh when Jim East, a man he had known from Tascosa, Texas, and another posse member transported them to Maxwell's house. "The Indian was wearing a scarf that she had made from angora goat hair," said Roberts. "I traded her my tintype picture in my shirt pocket for this scarf."

In 1949, W. H. Burges of El Paso, Texas, brought forth a letter written to him by the same Jim East on May 20, 1926. In the letter, East wrote that he and deputy Lee Hall were responsible for bringing the prisoners to Fort Sumner. He said that Mrs. Maxwell sent "the old Navajo woman over with a request to Captain Garrett to allow Billy to be sent over to her house so that her daughter Paulita and she could bid him good-by." When they arrived, Mrs. Maxwell asked the deputies to unlock the Kid from Rudabaugh and allow Paulita go into another room with him for an affectionate farewell. "But of course," wrote East, "we had to refuse."

The tintype to which Roberts referred was the only known photograph of Billy the Kid. The scarf that Roberts claimed he received in exchange for the picture was still in his possession at the time of his death.

Seven decades later, in 1949, Roberts recalled a relatively minor incident of which researchers were unaware and of which he appeared to be aware of many obscure details. The details were written down by Jim East twenty-three years earlier in a private letter to a man unknown to Roberts.

Severo Gallegos

When Roberts was recalling his escape from the Lincoln County jail, he related yet another minor incident. He told Morrison that after leaving the building, he came out into the street and climbed onto the horse that was waiting for him. Almost immediately, he slid off the opposite side and "hung onto the rope." Roberts stated that the "Gallegos kid went down the road and took a rope off a yoke of steers in the field and tied the rope to my saddle." Following this, the Kid rode away.

On October 11, 1949, during an interview with Severo Gallegos, the eighty-four-year-old resident of Ruidoso, New Mexico, told Morrison that on the afternoon of April 28, 1881, he and two young friends were playing marbles under a tree near the Lincoln County jail when Deputy Bell staggered out of the side door and fell dead. Moments later, the boys watched as Deputy Olinger was gunned down by Billy the Kid from the second-floor window. In a signed and notarized document, Gallegos stated that he and his friend were scared and that they ran but returned when the Kid called out to them and asked them to fetch a horse. After saddling the horse, explained Gallegos, jail cook Godfrey Gauss led it around to the front of the building and tied it to a hitching post. Gallegos recalled that as the Kid mounted the animal, he fell off the other side. "He told me to go down the road and get that rope from Priciliano, who had a rope tied over the horns of a cow. . . . I tied it around the neck of the horse and threw it on the saddle horn."

The event concerning the horse and the rope during the Kid's escape from the Lincoln County jail was never recorded by historians; yet, sixty-eight years later, the only two men still alive in 1949 who were participants described it in exactly the same way.

Mrs. Bernardo Salazar

Roberts recalled that, after fleeing from Lincoln after killing Bell and Olinger, he traveled west, entered a canyon, and went to the "home of a friend, who cut the bolts in my leg irons." After riding in a car with Morrison up the same canyon nearly seventy years later, Roberts said that after the irons were removed, he hid in the nearby brush, afraid that a posse might come to the friend's house. He said that Yginio Salazar brought him a blanket and some food.

On October 11, 1949, Mrs. Bernardo Salazar, the adopted daughter of Yginio Salazar, told Morrison that Yginio's cousin Cipio Salazar "cut the bolts and hid the irons." The next morning, she said, Yginio was riding a horse when he heard Billy whistle from the ditch. Yginio took the "saddle blanket off . . . and gave it to Billy to sleep on."

PERSONAL IDENTIFICATION

Henry H. Anthony

In 1945, Henry H. Anthony, a retired lawman who served with the Pinkerton Detective Agency and as a federal marshall, identified William Henry Roberts as Billy the Kid. In a letter dated August 27, 1990, James Anthony, grandson to Henry, recalled a 1945 incident in Hico, Texas. James Anthony, with his two younger brothers, his father, and his grandfather Henry, had walked into town to purchase some groceries and get haircuts. Grandfather Henry always carried a .45-caliber revolver everywhere he went, a habit he picked up while serving with the Pinkertons. As the men and boys waited their turn on a bench outside the barbershop, they noticed a man approximately the age of Henry Anthony walking toward them. The man was William Henry Roberts.

As the elder Anthony watched the approaching figure, he grew nervous and agitated. When Roberts was within fifteen feet of the group, Henry Anthony jumped up and cried, "Bonney . . . you're under arrest." When James Anthony's father tried to restrain the old man, the former marshal stated, "I'd know that son of a bitch Will Bonney anywhere. Ask him if I wouldn't." At this point, Roberts turned and ran back down the street while the family members made the elder Anthony return to the bench. For the rest of his life, Henry Anthony swore that the man he encountered on the Hico street was Billy the Kid and that he knew him from the "ranch wars."

During the years 1950 and 1951, there were a few people still living who had known the outlaw Billy the Kid. They included Severo Gallegos, Martile Able, Jose B. Montoya, Dewitt Travis, and Robert E. Lee. Each of these five people was introduced to William Henry Roberts by Morrison; each identified him as the Kid; and each committed his position to a signed and notarized affidavit. Among the papers left by Bill Allison, the stepgrandson of Roberts, were copies of five affidavits, each one testifying to the fact that Roberts was indeed the Kid.

Severo Gallegos

Severo Gallegos had known Billy the Kid, and in 1950 the eighty-four-year-old New Mexico resident was listed by attorneys of El Paso's Ted Andress law firm as a person who could testify that the outlaw was still alive. Gallegos, a half brother to Florencio Chavez who had a minor role in the Lincoln County War, played a small part in the outlaw's escape from the Lincoln County jail.

Morrison alone visited Gallegos at his home in Ruidoso in 1949. After talking with him for a while and establishing his connection to the Lincoln County of the previous century, Morrison invited the old man to return with him to his hotel room, where, he said, there was someone he wanted him to meet.

When the two men arrived at the hotel, Morrison introduced Roberts to Gallegos as William H. Bonney. According to Morrison, Gallegos seemed spellbound as he stared at and spoke with Roberts for several hours. When Gallegos was ready to leave, he told Morrison that he was skeptical about the identity of this man who called himself Roberts.

The following morning, Morrison went to the Gallegos home to see if he felt differently after having had time to think about his visit with Roberts. Gallegos told Morrison, "Your man talks like Billy; he looks like Billy; he has small hands and large wrists, small feet, large ears, stands and walks like Billy; but he is not old enough to be Billy the Kid."

Gallegos then told Morrison that if he could look into Roberts's eyes, he would be able to tell for certain whether the man was actually the Kid. "Billy had small brown spots in the blue of his eyes." If Roberts had the same brown spots, then Gallegos would say that Roberts was Billy the Kid.

Morrison admitted that, at the time, he had never noticed this feature of Roberts's eyes but told Gallegos he could have one more look. When they returned to the hotel room, Morrison asked Roberts to open the window and stand in the light so that Gallegos could examine him. Gallegos stared intently at Roberts's eyes for several seconds, turned to Morrison, and said, "That is Billy the Kid, all right. Only Billy has eyes like that. I am ready to swear that this man is Billy the Kid."

In an affidavit made on November 11, 1950, before a Lincoln County notary public, Gallegos stated that the Kid visited the Gallegos home in San Patricio on several occasions, ate many meals there, and that the Kid and Chavez did a lot of target practice together. Gallegos further stated that "Billy the Kid was a small man; that he had small feet and hands with large wrists; that he had two large teeth in front of his mouth; that he had blue-grey eyes with small brown spots in them; that his nose was straight, high cheekbones and large ears." Gallegos said that Roberts had the same bluegrey eyes with brown spots, the same nose, the same cheek bones, the large ears, the small feet, and the small hands with large wrists.

Furthermore, he said that Roberts talks and laughs the same and looks the same in many ways, except he no longer has the large teeth. Gallegos also stated that he made several visits to the Lincoln County jail when the Kid was chained there, to bring him food, and that he watched the Kid escape. In his affadavit, Gallegos states that he had not seen the Kid since the flight from Lincoln in 1881 until April 1, 1950, when he met William Henry Roberts. After visiting and talking with Roberts for several hours, Gallegos said he was convinced Roberts was the Kid.

Gallegos further states that he "never believed Billy the Kid was killed by sheriff Pat Garrett" and that he heard from time to time throughout the years that the Kid was still living. He concludes the affidavit by saying that he is "of the firm belief that Billy the Kid and Roberts is one and the same person."

Martile Able

According to Martile Able, she and her husband, John, knew Billy the Kid well. To substantiate her claim, which she made in 1950, she produced a photograph for Morrison, one taken in a barbershop. In the picture, John Able, the barber, is shaving a man in the chair. Mrs. Able said that Billy the Kid is seated on a nearby bench, waiting for a haircut. Mrs. Able claimed that she and her husband, who died in 1918, had spent time with the Kid on several occasions and that John had provided Billy with horses.

In 1950, Morrison brought Roberts to El Paso to meet Mrs. Able. When she was pointed out to him, Morrison asked Roberts: "Do you know this lady?" Roberts responded without hesitation saying, "Sure, that's John Able's wife." When Mrs. Able was introduced to William Henry Roberts, she immediately recognized him as Billy the Kid. "I knew him the moment I saw him," she said.

A few days later, on August 1, 1950, Mrs. Able signed an affidavit stating that Roberts was Billy the Kid. In the document, Able states that her family knew the Kid in Pecos, Texas, and that he visited with the Ables before and after his reported death at the hands of Pat Garrett. Able further states that her husband brought the Kid home with him one day and that she cooked him a meal. John Able loaned him a horse, and the Kid rode away the next day. The last time Mrs. Able saw Billy the Kid was in 1902, until she was reintroduced to him by Morrison in 1950.

Able contends in the affidavit that Roberts "laughs much the same . . . has the same keen, blue eyes, long nose, large ears, small feet, small hands with unusually large wrists, stands and walks as straight as ever with a lively step." Able states that "it was generally known among friends that Billy the Kid was not killed by Garrett in New Mexico, like they said he was killed; that Billy escaped into Mexico."

Jose B. Montoya

Jose B. Montoya was eleven years old at the time of the shooting at Fort Sumner. He was, he claimed, well acquainted with Billy the Kid, sheriff Pat Garrett, and deputy John Poe.

The Kid often stayed at the home of Montoya's family in the Capitan Mountains, outside of the town of Lincoln. Montoya described the Kid as having "large ears, a long straight nose, big teeth, small feet, small hands with large wrists off of which he could slip handcuffs." He said that the Kid "stood as straight as an arrow . . . was a good dancer and singer."

In a signed and notarized affidavit on February 13, 1951, in Lincoln County, Montoya states that he did "not believe the story of Garrett killing the Kid" and that he and another man, named Green, saw Billy the Kid at a bullfight in Juarez, Mexico, in 1902, and both of them knew the Kid. Montoya concludes that William Henry Roberts and Billy the Kid are the same man.

Dewitt Travis

Dewitt Travis knew William Henry Roberts since early childhood and maintained all his life that he and Billy the Kid were the same man.

In a notarized affidavit dated December 12, 1951, at Gregg County, Texas, Travis described Roberts as standing "about five feet and eight inches, weighing about one hundred and sixty-five pounds in later years" and "fair complected with high cheekbones, long straight nose, large ears with the left ear protruding farther away from the head than the right ear, blue-grey eyes keen and shifty, with dark hair graying in later years, peculiarly shaped teeth protruding outward from under the upper lip." The teeth, according to Travis, were extracted by a Dr. Cruz in Gladewater, Texas, in 1931.

According to Travis, Roberts wore a size-seven boot and had small hands with large wrists. He was "very muscular, quick as lightning, calm and collected . . . quick on the draw," and could shoot a pistol either right- or left-handed.

Travis also verified that the Kid returned to Texas from Mexico around 1884 and called himself the Texas Kid and that while working for the Anti-Horsethief Association near Hugo, Oklahoma, he went by the name of Hugo Kid. Travis also acknowledged that Roberts rode in Wild West shows with Buffalo Bill and Pawnee Bill and that he had lived in Arkansas and Oklahoma as well as Texas.

Travis maintained that Roberts seldom admitted he was Billy the Kid to anyone until shortly before his death but that his few close friends always knew he was the famous outlaw. In the affidavit, Travis states that William Henry Roberts and Billy the Kid are "one and the same person" and that the Kid was not killed by Pat Garrett in Fort Sumner on July 14, 1881.

Robert E. Lee

On July 5, 1950, Robert E. Lee of Baton Rouge, Louisiana, signed a notarized affidavit that reveals the extent of his relationship with William Henry Roberts.

Lee, who worked as a guard for Buffalo Bill's Wild West Show, says that it was generally known to him and others that Billy the Kid "was not killed by Pat Garrett in 1881 . . . that the Kid escaped from Fort Sumner into Old Mexico and lived with the Yaqui Indians in Sonora," and that he "assumed the name the Texas Kid when he returned to this country." Lee further states in his affidavit that the "Kid . . . was riding in Buffalo Bill's Wild West Show in Chicago, Illinois, in 1893." Lee says that the Kid's father, Wild Henry Roberts, fought Indians with Buffalo Bill and that the showman hired the Kid because he was well acquainted with the Roberts family.

Lee confirmed that Roberts was the man known as Billy the Kid; that he stands about five feet, eight inches; that he has "blue eyes with hazel spots in them, large ears"; and that the buck teeth "are no longer in his mouth." Affiant Lee further states that "Billy the Kid was not killed by Pat Garrett at Maxwell's home in Fort Sumner, New Mexico, on July 14, 1881."

To have an affidavit notarized requires no proof of what has been stated, only that the statement is witnessed by an authorized person. A few who oppose Roberts's identity as Billy the Kid have criticized the five affidavits and maintain that they have no credibility. Unexplained, however, is how and why five individuals who knew Roberts as Billy the Kid, most of whom did not know one another and had nothing to gain, would insist that the two were the same man.

Yginio Salazar

Yginio Salazar rode with Billy the Kid during the Lincoln County War and was said by some to be as close to the young outlaw as anyone.

During an interview in the 1930s with author Miguel Antonio Otero, Salazar stated that he knew "many people . . . who saw Billy's body after Pat Garrett killed him."

To his death, however, Salazar maintained to others that the "killing" of the Kid by Garrett was a hoax and that close friends of the Kid were involved in a cover-up. Salazar claimed at one time to have received a letter from the Kid telling him the truth of what happened in Fort Sumner the night of July 14, 1881, when Garrett allegedly shot and killed the outlaw. According to grandson Joe Salazar, William Henry Roberts, alias Billy the Kid, returned to Lincoln in 1932 and 1948 to visit Yginio.

Those who knew Salazar believed that he talked very little to outsiders about the Kid because he was trying to protect him. C. L. Sonnichsen stated that Salazar always believed the Kid was alive.

Cain Letter

In a March 26, 1983, letter to a woman named Ola Everhard, Paul Cain of Victoria, Texas, told her that he had recently met one of Pat Garrett's daughters in Roswell, New Mexico. Though blind, the daughter taught piano to youth. The daughter told Cain that "her dad did not kill Billy the Kid as they were good friends."

George Coe

George Coe, with his cousin Frank, rode and fought with Billy the Kid during the days of the Lincoln County War; was wounded in the fight at Blazer's Mill; and became a successful rancher in the area. Coe often told interviewers that it was not the Kid who was killed by Garrett.

THE UNIVERSITY OF TEXAS PHOTO-COMPARISON ANALYSIS

With the passage of time from the alleged killing of Billy the Kid in 1881 to the present, definitive proof that William Henry Roberts and Billy the Kid were the same man is not likely possible. The evidence that the two could be the same—Morrison's findings, Roberts's recollections, personal identifications, and Roberts's uncanny physical similarity to Billy the Kid—is striking and compelling; yet, like the accounts of the killing as related by Pat Garrett and the swarm of writers that followed him, this remains evidence, not proof.

During the 1940s and 1950s, computer technology that could compare images such as the tintype of Billy the Kid with a likeness of William Henry Roberts was not available. Since the 1970s, however, computers and attendant hardware and software have been developed with this capability. At least two tested, validated, and statistically proven systems for facial pattern recognition have come into common usage by law enforcement organizations worldwide, thus enabling the CIA, the FBI, Interpol, Scotland Yard, and other law enforcement agencies to identify criminals and missing persons despite disguises and changes due to age and surgery. Facial-pattern recognition systems developed as early as 1972 (see Kaya and Kobayashi) have a statistical reliability so that 92 percent of the time the computer cannot be fooled by disguises, facial hair, age, or cosmetic alterations.

In the recent past, a number of comparisons have been made between photographs of William Henry Roberts and what has been called the Dedrick–Upham tintype, the only authenticated image of Billy the Kid. Most of these comparisons were poorly disguised attempts to discredit Roberts. A legitimate, scientifically based and statistically significant photo-comparison analysis was finally undertaken in 1990 at the University of Texas at Austin. Unlike earlier studies that attempted to prove Roberts was not Billy the Kid, the Texas study was undertaken with no preconceived notions whatsoever, only scientific objectivity and the truth.

The study, conducted at the Laboratory for Vision Studies and the Advanced Graphic Laboratory at the University of Texas, Austin, was supervised by Dr. Alan Bovik of the Department of Electrical and Computer Engineering. Bovik was assisted by Scott Acton, who received his doctorate a short time later. In addition to a copy of the Billy the Kid tintype and a comparable image of William Henry Roberts, two additional photographs—one identified as a "young Henry McCarty" and the other alleged to be a "young William Henry Roberts"—were included for comparison purposes. In 1990, the University of Texas Laboratory for Vision Systems maintained state-of-the-art facilities and equipment—computers, cameras, processors, monitors, and printers—for such studies.

The photographs were digitized and image improved by employing a variety of image-processing techniques. The four photographs were searched for similarities and differences, with the focus being on facial features that criminologists employ in their identification of suspects.

The most important part of the study involved a computerized recognition system. According to Acton, the fundamental research

and design of the system used was from Townes (1976) and Kaya and
Kobayashi (1972). Hundreds of studies conducted by the FBI, CIA,
Interpol, and Scotland Yard employing these techniques have yielded
an impressive success rate in face recognition, thus providing for a
significant level of statistical validity.

The process involved scanning and digitizing the four photographs
into a 512-by-512-byte image, computing the LoG (Laplacian of a
Gaussian) edgemap, identifying reference points such as jaw width and
internal and external biocular points, determining the distances between
the features, and finally computing an error estimate for the match.

The technicians at the Laboratory for Vision Systems used nine
features selected from the Kaya and Kobayashi method. Distances
between features were all normalized so that the distance between
the exact center of the eyeballs in each image, or intrapupillary distance, was one hundred pixels, or picture elements. All subsequent
measurements were likewise in pixels and relative to the intrapupillary distance.

In addition to the intrapupillary distance, the features measured
were internal biocular breadth, or distance between the inside of the
eyes; external biocular breadth, or distance between the outside of the
eyes; nose breadth, or width of the nose measured from the outside of
the nostrils; mouth breadth; bizygomatic breadth, or width of the
cheek bones measured with a line running just under the nose;
midlip-to-chin distance; midlip-to-nose distance; and nose length.
Bigonial breadth, or width of the jaw measured in a line running hor-
izontally across the mouth, was not employed due to the difficulty encountered in precisely locating the endpoints in the tintype.

For each image, the normalized feature measurements were listed,
and a mean-squared error for each was established, all in comparison
to the authenticated tintype. The lower the mean-squared error
(MSE), the better the match.

The measurements for the Billy the Kid tintype, in pixels, were cal-
culated. The MSE from the tintype, compared to itself, would yield
zero, an exact match. The measurements for the alleged photographs
of "a young Henry McCarty" and a "young William Henry Roberts"
yielded MSEs of 29.3 and 79.6, respectively, each large enough, according to the analysts, to reject both images as being Billy the Kid.
Analyst Acton explained that the young Henry McCarty image is the
face of a male that has not yet reached maturity, with the skull not
fully developed; thus, it could not be expected to match up statistically with the Billy the Kid image. The alleged "young William Henry

Roberts" image later turned out to be a photograph not of Roberts at all but of a relative. The photograph of William Henry Roberts that was employed, one taken when he was in his late eighties and one in which the camera-facing position is comparable to that of the tintype, yielded some provocative measurements when compared to those of Billy the Kid (see table 11.1).Compared to the Billy the Kid tintype, Roberts's measurements manifest a remarkable similarity and yield an MSE of only 17.7, low enough, according to the analysts, to suggest a match.

When the analysis was completed, researcher Frederic Bean was contacted by one of the investigators and invited to come to the laboratory and view the results. Because of a scheduling conflict, Bean initially declined but was encouraged to change his mind by the researcher, who told him it might be important "because you are getting ready to rewrite history." In his report, analyst Acton stated, "The similarity between the facial structures of . . . Roberts and the man in the . . . tintype is indeed amazing."

The only source of significant error between the two images is related to the bizygomatic breadth. This distance, it was explained, can increase with weight gain. According to Acton, "The picture of Roberts shows more body fat than the man in the tintype." The slight difference in the midlip-to-chin distance, said Acton, can easily be accounted for by dental work—that is, Roberts had no teeth when the photograph was made.

Table 11.1   Photo comparison of William Henry Roberts and Billy the Kid

	Billy the Kid Tintype	William Henry Roberts
INTRAPUPILLARY DISTANCE	100	100
INTERNAL BIOCULAR BREADTH	67	67
EXTERNAL BIOCULAR BREADTH	137	133
NOSE BREADTH	55	51
MOUTH BREADTH	80	82
BIZYGOMATIC BREADTH	204	214
MIDLIP-TO-CHIN DISTANCE	72	73
MIDLIP-TO-NOSE DISTANCE	39	39
NOSE LENGTH	82	82

On March 1, 1996, the results of the University of Texas photo-comparison study, with other evidence, were presented to Andre McNeil, chancery judge of Arkansas's Twelfth Judicial District, and noted Arkansas attorney Helen Rice Grinder. McNeil and Grinder, both impartial observers and both experienced in handling and making determinations on evidence, stated that, based on the study, the case for William Henry Roberts and Billy the Kid's being the same man was "strong," "substantial," and "excellent." McNeil and Grinder maintained that while no legal determination would ever likely be made relative to the identity, they were "impressed with the study, along with the historical integrity of the accompanying documents."

The University of Texas photo-comparison study, the only valid one commissioned to date, adds another layer of evidence in support of the notion that Roberts and the Kid are the same person. In the words of the analysts, the study "irrefutably shows that Roberts and the Kid are a very close match" and that the similarity between the two is "amazing."

Any single piece of evidence purporting to show that William Henry Roberts and Billy the Kid are the same person, no matter how compelling, may not convince everyone. However, when one considers the entire body of evidence—the numerous uncanny physical similarities, Roberts's precise and detailed observations, the personal identifications, and the photo-comparison study—this preponderance of logical, verifiable, and powerful evidence cannot be ignored.

Did Pat Garrett kill Billy the Kid in Pete Maxwell's bedroom on the night of July 4, 1881? The evidence for such is inconsistent, contradictory, and inconclusive.

Was William Henry Roberts Billy the Kid? The evidence suggests that he was.

TWELVE

◆◆◆

An Opposing Point of View

When William V. Morrison took William Henry Roberts to Santa Fe in 1950 to meet with the governor of New Mexico regarding a petition for pardon, he initiated a surprising and intense level of resistance and criticism from many who held an opposing point of view, individuals who were convinced that the old man could not under any circumstances have been Billy the Kid. According to Morrison's notes on the meeting, Roberts was immediately labeled a fraud and an imposter by critics. Roberts was asked a number of questions that had nothing to do with his request for pardon. In several cases, his answers differed from the traditional versions of history, thereby inviting scorn and ridicule. In other cases, the terrified Roberts, fighting for equanimity, simply gave inadequate answers. The governor poked fun at Roberts. Garrett descendants and a squad of armed guards intimidated him. Not only was the gathering a transparent attempt to discredit Roberts, but it was also a media opportunity for the governor. Roberts was never given a chance to tell his story as he had been promised, and Morrison was never allowed to submit the evidential documents he brought along.

Criticism and resistance related to the idea that Roberts was Billy the Kid were invited and accommodated, but no one stepped forward with logical, substantive, and defensible evidence to suggest that Roberts was mistaken. The principal fault they found with him was the fact that his answers to questions did not agree with the published history. A month later, Roberts died without receiving an opportunity to present his case.

In 1955, *Alias Billy the Kid*, by Sonnichesen and Morrison, was released. Roberts's story was told, allowing for the possibility that he could have been Billy the Kid. After reading *Alias*, many were convinced, based on the evidence presented, that Roberts could have been the outlaw. Others insisted that there was not enough adequate documentation to support the hypothesis. As a result of the book, Roberts was attacked posthumously by the traditionalists and again branded as a fraud. Some holding strong opposition to Roberts's claims attacked Morrison, who was accused of being an opportunist. Even Dr. Sonnichsen became a target for members of the anti-Roberts camp, who faulted him for writing the book. A number of Billy the Kid enthusiasts vilified Sonnichsen, disregarding the fact that the book made no claims at all, only suggestions.

While none of the anti-Roberts faction adequately addressed any of the evidence presented in *Alias Billy the Kid*, during subsequent years they tendered a number of opinions representing an opposing point of view via reviews and other published material as well as personal letters, all of which invite response.

1. Roberts's handwriting does not match that of Billy the Kid. The truth is that no one knows what Billy the Kid's handwriting looks like. The Kid received little formal education, so his reading and writing skills were rudimentary. Copies of letters attributed to Billy the Kid were submitted to prominent handwriting analyst Howard Chandler, former director of the Arkansas state police and one of the country's leading forensic handwriting analysts. According to Chandler, the well-crafted and artfully constructed letters attributed to Billy the Kid were written by at least two men, probably law clerks who moonlighted as scribes for a small fee, taking dictation from those who were unable to write themselves. There exists no pertinent evidence that Billy the Kid wrote the letters attributed to him.

2. William Henry Roberts's real name was Oliver P. Roberts, a man whose history does not resemble that claimed by William Henry. Author Frederick Nolan claims, "There is one final, irrefutable, unavoidable fact which . . . utterly destroys any claim" that Roberts might be Billy the Kid, a "single, unassailable piece of documentary evidence." Nolan is referring to what he calls the "Roberts family Bible." According to a woman Nolan identifies as Roberts's niece, the Bible says that the "third child of Henry O. Roberts and his second wife S. E. Ferguson . . . was a son, Oliver P. Roberts, born August 26, 1879."

In 1988, researcher and writer William A. Tunstill mistakenly identified William Henry Roberts as Oliver P. Roberts. Since then, others attempting to discredit William Henry have parroted this error. Oliver Pleasant Roberts, a cousin, was born in 1879 in Arkansas and married a woman named Anna, all of which is documented by the family Bible mentioned by Nolan, as well as by a marriage certificate and by census records. This Bible mentioned by Nolan belonged to the family of Henry Oliver Roberts, the brother of James Henry and uncle to William Henry Roberts, alias Billy the Kid. It contains little pertinent information about James Henry's descendants.

William Henry Roberts had no nieces. The family Bible that was in the possession of William Henry Roberts when he died had its origins with the family of James Henry Roberts. It was passed on to William Henry's widow, Melinda, later to her grandson Bill Allison, and is currently in the possession of his descendants. This Bible lists William Henry Roberts's birth date as December 31, 1859.

For most of his life, William Henry Roberts used the alias Oliver L. but never Oliver P. Moreover, handwriting analyses of William Henry and Oliver Pleasant leave no doubt that the two men are indeed two different persons.

3. There is no record of a William Henry Roberts in Lincoln County between 1878 and 1881. Roberts was using the aliases William Bonney, Henry McCarty, and Henry Antrim. Some anti-Roberts researchers claim that if his name was not on the census, then he could not have been there. Both the Lincoln County Historical Trust and the Billy the Kid Museum in Fort Sumner have in their collections photographs of men who resided in Lincoln and San Miguel Counties during the 1870s and 1880s that no one has identified to date.

4. Roberts claimed he was left-handed because the Kid was presumed by many to be left-handed. Roberts was ambidextrous, and he claimed both right- and left-handedness, a fact verified by those who knew him.

5. Deputies Poe and McKinney both concurred that Billy the Kid was slain by Pat Garrett on the night of July 14, 1881. Poe initially disagreed with Garrett but ultimately would have had no way of knowing since he had never seen the Kid. He simply went along with what Garrett told him. McKinney, who some suspected knew the Kid slightly, also went along with Garrett at the time. McKinney, however, was quoted years later stating that Garrett did not kill the Billy the Kid.

6. Critics point out that Roberts claimed that the man Garrett killed was Billy Barlow, a person who has never been noted in any

Lincoln County census records. If Barlow had arrived in Lincoln County between census takings, he would not have been listed. Barlow may have been using an alias and may have been in the census records under another name.

7. *Billy the Kid spoke fluent Spanish, but Roberts did not.* Roberts lived in rural parts of Mexico off and on for a few years, and it is inconceivable that he didn't pick up the language. According to copies of letters written by Morrison, Roberts spoke a "passable" Spanish. When Roberts met and visited with Severo Gallegos in 1950, much of their conversation, according to Morrison, was conducted in Spanish. Sonnichsen also verified that Roberts spoke Spanish.

8. *There is no record of William Henry Roberts serving with Teddy Roosevelt's Rough Riders.* There exists no record of the name William Henry Roberts in the records of those who served in the campaign nor any of Roberts's other known aliases. No one knows which alias he used when he enlisted.

9. *Researcher Donald Cline insists that Roberts could not have served with the Anti-Horsethief Association since that agency never existed.* Records pertaining to the Anti-Horsethief Association are on file at the Western Collections Library at the University of Oklahoma. At the time of his death, in 1950, Roberts was in possession of an official Anti-Horsethief Association badge as well as an old photograph showing him astride a horse bearing the association's brand.

10. *Billy the Kid had buck teeth, but no photo of Roberts shows prominent front incisors.* Most authenticated photographs of Roberts were made at a late age when he had no teeth, his two upper incisors having been extracted in 1931 and the rest in ensuing years. A few photos purported to be of a young Roberts, photos that might indicate buck teeth, have never been authenticated.

11. *Pat Garrett and deputy John Poe agreed that the man slain in Maxwell's bedroom was Billy the Kid, and the two men wrote about the killing saying roughly the same thing.* The accounts of Garrett and Poe reveal several glaring discrepancies about what occurred that night. Author Leon Metz points out that Garrett could have passed off any corpse as that of Billy the Kid, and Poe would not have known since he had never laid eyes on the outlaw.

12. William V. Morrison, the man who found Roberts, was a fraud because he claimed to be a lawyer when in fact he was not. Morrison never claimed to be a lawyer. He did claim to be an attorney, which he was. An attorney is a person who is legally appointed to transact business for another. An attorney can be a lawyer and normally is, but such is not required. Morrison worked part-time for law firms as a paralegal, a job that consisted of a number of clerical duties and footwork as it related to bankruptcy, wills, and other cases. He took paralegal correspondence courses from and received a degree from LaSalle College in Chicago. He also took extension courses in bankruptcy.

None of the above arguments is persuasive enough to make one reject William Henry Roberts as Billy the Kid. To date, no one has proven that William Henry Roberts's claims were contrived.

THE LINCOLN COUNTY HISTORICAL TRUST PHOTO-COMPARISON STUDY

The Lincoln County Historical Trust (LCHT)—a private, nonprofit organization founded by a small group of businessmen, artists, and writers—has been operational since 1978. The stated goals of the trust are related to historical, cultural, and environmental preservation in Lincoln County, New Mexico. In the town of Lincoln, the trust operates a small museum, museum store, and visitor center.

In 1987, a man named Robert L. Hart was hired by the trust, and one of his first major activities was called the Billy the Kid photographic research project. According to Hart, it was intended to be "a multiyear disciplinary endeavor to investigate images of Billy the Kid." In 1988, the LCHT Board of Trustees formally approved the project.

Hart stated that all alleged photographs of Billy the Kid would be "subjected to painstaking historical research," which was described as applying measurements of points on the faces of images not readily dismissed as authentic Billy the Kid photographs. The images would then be compared to the Dedrick–Upham tintype. Selected to head the digital-processing and image-enhancement phase of the project was Dr. Thomas G. Kyle, a physicist employed by the Los Alamos National Laboratory, New Mexico. At the time, Kyle was attached to the Computer Research and Applications Group at the research facility. The Los Alamos National Laboratory is a facility owned by the U.S. Department of Energy and is operated by the University of California, with "nuclear weapon technology . . . the laboratory's primary focus." Hart claimed that the laboratory was enlisted as a project participant because of the "public relations value of work on local and regional history."

For this important research project, Kyle employed an Apple Macintosh II computer and created his own method for making photographic comparisons. For reasons known only to Kyle, he chose not to use existing statistically proven and court-approved photo-comparison techniques that had been available for at least seventeen years. According to Hart, William Henry Roberts "was to become the prime focus of attention with an immediate goal of project publicity." Kyle stated that the computer was to be used to compare certain facial characteristics of Billy the Kid and Roberts. For the Kid, the Dedrick–Upham tintype was employed; for Roberts, a frontal view taken in 1950 was used.

In a July 1990 article in *True West* magazine, Kyle states that both images were scaled to the same approximate size and "adjusted." Tilt of the head must also be accounted for, says Kyle, for "as the head is tilted, the relative position of the eyes and ears changes." The best way to correct this, he continues, is to draw horizontal lines "through the eyes and beneath the nose to indicate by how much the vertical measurements might be affected."

In comparing the photograph of Billy the Kid with the likeness of Roberts, "contrast and lighting level have been adjusted to make edges of the features, such as the eyes and chin, as sharply defined as possible." After ensuring that the images of the Kid and Roberts had the same magnification, by adjusting pupil width, Kyle explains that Roberts's "eyes are almost level with the top of his ears." Kyle then states that the "horizontal line that passes under Roberts's nose passes well below Billy's nose." In spite of the earlier acknowledgement that the tilt of the head can be important, Kyle goes on to say that "such a significant difference cannot be explained by the tilt."

In a second and rather curious measurement, Kyle drew two "identical boxes" on the chins of the images of the Kid and Roberts. The top of the box, he says, "is positioned at the horizontal dip in the chin, just below the gum line and low enough to be unaffected" by Roberts's missing teeth. The box was then applied to the Kid's chin. The same size box, said Kyle, came far below Roberts's chin because it was smaller. From this measurement, Kyle concludes that "the chins are different and that . . . Roberts and Billy the Kid were not the same person."

Kyle writes that the ears of the Kid and Roberts manifest even "greater differences than the chins" and that with increasing age "the lobe of the ear becomes larger, but the rest of the ear remains unchanged." According to Kyle's computer analysis of the ears of the Kid and Roberts, the two men are dramatically different.

Using Kyle's study, the Lincoln County Historical Trust, as well as some historians and a greater number of outlaw buffs, concluded that William Henry Roberts could not be Billy the Kid.

Elements of the LCHT photo-comparison analysis, ranging from motive to research design to conclusions, beg critical attention. First, the LCHT had a vested interest, not necessarily in the truth, but in Kyle's making the determination that Roberts was not the Kid. The study was commissioned by the trust, with members who are adherents to the version of history that claims Billy the Kid was killed and buried in Fort Sumner, New Mexico. The towns of Lincoln and Fort Sumner are major tourist attractions in the state, and Billy the Kid–related tourism and purchases amount to millions of dollars in revenue for New Mexico every year. To a large extent, the very existence of the trust depends in part on maintaining this historical status quo as it relates to Billy the Kid history.

Second, compared to extant, tested, and validated photo-comparison studies such as the one employed in the University of Texas analysis, Kyle's research design is surprisingly elementary and unworthy of agency involvement such as the Los Alamos National Laboratory. Shortly after the commencement of this project, Frederic Bean sent a letter to the agency questioning the elementary nature of the research as well as Kyle's lack of qualifications. The Los Alamos National Laboratory responded by informing Bean it was withdrawing official support of Kyle's involvement. Kyle continued his work with the project but in a private capacity.

Third, given the availability of a number of sophisticated computers and auxiliary equipment, the selection of an Apple Mcintosh II computer is puzzling. While a decent and effective home computer product, this machine lacked the precision and capacity necessary for a professional, statistically valid photo comparison.

Fourth, Kyle or anyone else wishing to make a valid computer photo comparison had at his disposal at least two statistically proven programs developed by Townes and the research team of Kaya and Kobayashi. Why these widely used and available programs were not employed in the study is puzzling.

Fifth, an examination of Kyle's study as it relates to the eyes and ears of the subjects suggests a loose interpretation of the results. In his analysis, Kyle states that in the Dedrick–Upham image, the horizontal line that runs between the pupils of Billy's eyes is located well above the top of his ears. In truth, the tops of the Kid's ears are lost in shadow or hair and cannot be seen. Furthermore, it is clear that the front-to-back tilt of the Kid's head, already acknowledged by Kyle, would have an important effect on the perceptual relationship between the eye and the ears. Kyle contradicts himself in his own study.

Kyle also states that the horizontal line between Roberts's pupils is "almost level with the top of his ears." Kyle's illustration, however, shows that the line is a long way from the top of Roberts's ears and that Roberts's head is tilted differently from the image in the Dedrick–Upham photograph.

Sixth, Kyle's evaluation of the measurements from the pupil line to the nose is also fraught with problems. He is incorrect when he states that the difference between the pupil line to the nose is not affected by the tilt of the head.

In Kyle's analysis of the graphic he designed, he points out that the horizontal line that passes immediately under Roberts's nose passes well below Billy's nose and that what he calls a "significant difference cannot be explained by the tilt of Billy's head." The most cursory examination of the images and the superimposed markings reveals that the line does not in fact "pass well below Billy's nose." There is only a mere fraction-of-an-inch difference between the location of the line and the nose. Kyle's interpretation is incorrect. Both Roberts and Billy the Kid had noses that were described as "long." When the Kid's head, or anyone else's, is tilted back, the level of the tip of the nose is elevated. When the head is straightened so that the subject is facing directly ahead, as in the case of the Roberts photograph, the tip of the nose is lowered.

Seventh, Kyle devotes some attention to what he considers significant differences in the ears of the two men. This focus is odd, since there are clear and apparent similarities between the ears of the Kid and Roberts. However, according to professional photo-comparison analyst Dr. Scott Acton, ears are rarely considered in any professional facial-comparison study.

The LCHT photo-comparison study lacks validity and credibility. What remains baffling is that the LCHT, as well as a handful of historians and Billy the Kid enthusiasts, embraced these results without question.

THIRTEEN

The New Mexico Resistance

The state of New Mexico, a land of scenic beauty and a national leader in the arts, culture, and education, figures prominently in the Billy the Kid controversy.

New Mexico is justifiably proud of its history and has a vested interest in supporting and promoting the traditional tale of Billy the Kid. A significant portion of southeastern New Mexico called "Billy the Kid Country" is touted by billboards throughout the region. There is even a route passing through Lincoln and Ruidoso that is identified as the "Billy the Kid National Scenic Byway." It is publicized most in Ruidoso, a town the Kid passed through a few times and the home of ski resorts, condominium development, a race track, and other important tourist attractions. In Lincoln, visitors walk the same streets as the Kid and Pat Garrett and can examine displays at the old Lincoln County Courthouse. Though not part of the scenic byway, Fort Sumner attracts tourists who visit the alleged grave, purchase souvenirs at museum stores, order a Biscuit McKid at a local restaurant, and stay at a local motel named the Billy the Kid Motor Inn. Not far away can be found other favored tourist destinations, such as Carlsbad Caverns and White Sands National Monument.

To New Mexico residents and retailers, Billy the Kid represents business worth several million dollars each year, an issue important to elected politicians, up to the office of governor. State officials and business leaders have expressed concern that if William Henry Roberts, born Texan and died Texan, were Billy the Kid, it could have a negative impact on a portion of the state's economy.

An example of this perpetuation is the alleged gravesite of Billy the Kid. The majority of tourists who visit the location each year believe the Kid lies beneath the marker. Though significant doubts have been raised, the assumption continues to be advanced by economic interests.

Lincoln and Fort Sumner were Billy the Kid–related tourist destinations for many years before the discovery of William Henry Roberts. New Mexico governor Thomas G. Mabry, whose office oversaw tourism in New Mexico in 1950, was sensitive to the impact Roberts's claim might have had on state business.

Mabry had promised Roberts's representative, William V. Morrison, a private legal hearing. In a letter to Billy the Kid historian Philip J. Rasch, Morrison explained that at the capitol, as he attended to Roberts during a moment of illness that appeared to be a heart attack, Mabry was led into a private room by General Pat Hurley, a politician with strong New Mexico ties. Hurley was the nephew of John Hurley, who fought against the Kid during the Lincoln County War. When Mabry and Hurley finally emerged from the room following their conference, the governor announced to reporters that he had changed his mind and would not consider a pardon for Roberts. Morrison stated his belief that Hurley convinced the governor that tampering with the traditional Billy the Kid story might have dire consequences for the state's tourist industry and lead to voters rejecting Mabry at the next election.

The meeting between Roberts and Mabry turned into a farce characterized by one-sidedness. Opponents to the proposition that Roberts might be the Kid introduced unrelated matters, and Mabry refused to look at the numerous supporting documents brought to Santa Fe by Morrison.

The presence of Oscar and Jarvis Garrett, sons of the late sheriff Pat Garrett—with descendants of George Coe, Thomas McKinney, and Sheriff Brady (the man the Kid allegedly killed and for whose death he was sentenced to hang)—carried an intense level of intimidation for the ninety-year-old Roberts. The presence of the Eddy County sheriff and a large number of state troopers was disorienting and intimidating for Roberts.

Following Roberts's death, in 1950, some of the momentum about the contention he might be Billy the Kid died. In 1955, the publication of *Alias Billy the Kid* rekindled interest for a time. During the subsequent decades, continued and persistent examination of the text of *Alias* caused many to ponder the revelations of William Henry Roberts, several of which were subsequently supported by documentation. The book, as well as the continued interest in Billy the Kid lore and legend, also renewed efforts by a few traditionalists who supported the status quo. New Mexico citizens and politicians entered the fray and added to the criticism, but no one ever presented any actual evidence showing Roberts was not the Kid.

When clearer interpretations of the facts surrounding William Henry Roberts, as well as new ones, began to surface—in particular, the results of the University of Texas photo-comparison study in 1990—efforts to denounce Roberts were revived by some who possessed strong New Mexico connections. One of the attempts was the Lincoln County Historical Trust–sponsored photo-comparison study. Another example of resistance to the position of William Henry Roberts as Billy the Kid occurred at a symposium sponsored September 11–15, 1991, by the Lincoln County Historical Trust titled "In the Days of Billy the Kid: Violence and the Western Frontier."

One of the symposium's scheduled panels centered on the LCHT photo-comparison study and another conducted by Lewis Sadler. Representing the LCHT, Sadler chose to ignore the only two widely used, statistically valid, and available studies and designed one of his own. Despite the fact that his analysis lacked any statistical validity, one of the symposium participants, Jerry Weddle, told those in attendance that "extensive computer analysis of the only authenticated tintype of Billy and photographs of Roberts leave no doubt that they were two different men." To anyone with knowledge of professional photo-comparison analyses, it left nothing but doubt.

William A. Tunstill, an independent researcher who believes Roberts was Billy the Kid, was known to LCHT director Hart but was not invited to the symposium. Tunstill requested a meeting with LCHT officials but was denied. He challenged the positions of the LCHT and the faculty and invited them to provide valid evidence for their stated positions. In fact, Tunstill offered $10,000 if trust officials could submit proof that Pat Garrett killed Billy the Kid. To date, no one has claimed the reward.

Yet another New Mexico–related attempt to remove Roberts from consideration as Billy the Kid was televised on the ABC News program *Prime Time Live*.

In a segment titled "Who Was Billy the Kid?" cohost Sam Donaldson acknowledged the economic benefits that Lincoln and DeBaca Counties and the state of New Mexico reaped from the legend. Donaldson called it "the marketing of the Kid" and stated that in Fort Sumner "it's a business that draws 8,400 visitors a year and half-a-million dollars in revenue." If Roberts were found to be Billy the Kid, said Donaldson, it could "rob this town of its livelihood." A Fort Sumner businessman named Don Sweet, interviewed for the episode, stated that "this is getting very, very serious, and it has come to a point where economics is involved." Toward the end of the televised segment, Donaldson featured Sadler, who discussed his computer program and insisted that his findings invalidated Roberts's claims to Kid status.

Other than the bogus photo-comparison study, not a single piece of evidence was presented that could disprove that Roberts might be the Kid. Donaldson even confused William Henry Roberts with Oliver P. Roberts. At the end of the program, Donaldson turned to the camera and concluded that Roberts "is not Billy the Kid."

Like the LCHT study and the subsequent symposium, the *Prime Time Live* segment was inclined toward convincing viewers that William Henry Roberts could not be Billy the Kid. Unknown to viewers was the fact that Sam Donaldson owned a home and property in Lincoln County, New Mexico.

Yet another New Mexico governor has joined the Billy the Kid controversy. Governor Bill Richardson made national headlines in early 2003 as a result of spearheading an effort to change the designation of Route 666, which runs through New Mexico, Colorado, and Utah, to Route 491. Richardson argued that the biblical link between the number 666 and Satan was threatening the economic well-being of the towns along the route. According to the Book of Revelation (13:11), a ram-horned, dragonlike beast would stamp 666 on foreheads and hands, the so-called mark of the beast, designating the bearer as Satan or one of his minions. The passage does not mention New Mexico's highways.

In May 2003, Lincoln County sheriff Tom Sullivan announced that his office, with help from the state of New Mexico, "will use 21st-century technology to hopefully put to rest questions about what actually happened at the shooting in 1881." Sullivan says that "DNA testing can prove where the body of the real Billy the Kid rests and that sheriff Pat Garrett shot him dead on July 14, 1881, in a house in Fort Sumner, New Mexico." Before turning a single spadeful of dirt, Sullivan has already reached a conclusion.

Sullivan claimed he had "the go-ahead from the family to exhume the body of the Kid's mother," who is buried in Silver City. Sullivan has two important problems ahead of him. He cannot be absolutely certain that the body he wishes to exhume is that of the Kid's mother and not his aunt. Sullivan, like many of the Billy the Kid enthusiasts, is relying on lore, not fact. Additionally, since the headstone for Catherine Antrim has been moved, how can he be certain that it is indeed Ms. Antrim who lies beneath it? The actual location of her grave has been in question for decades.

Part of the investigation also involves digging up the body of Roberts, whom Sullivan insists "was buried in Hico, Texas." Exhumation might take awhile, since Roberts is buried in Hamilton, Texas.

Not to be outdone, and finding an opportunity for easy publicity, Governor Richardson scheduled a press conference in June 2003 to "detail how the state will aid" Sullivan's investigation. According to Richardson, "The reputation of Pat Garrett . . . hangs in the balance." Garrett's image is on the shoulder patch of Lincoln County deputies.

Robert Utley, author of *Billy the Kid: A Short and Violent Life*, states that "the investigation is doomed" and that it is "all just an exercise in publicity." Nolan refers to the governor's activity as a "circus" and claims "tourism may be the real reason behind renewed scrutiny."

Logically, the investigators would seek to dig up the Fort Sumner grave of Billy the Kid, but it is doubtful they will tamper with the alleged site since doing so might prove to the public it is a fake. In fear that such a thing might happen, the Fort Sumner city council met and "unanimously opposed any attempt to dig up the grave." Richardson stated, "The benefits to our state and to the history of the West far outweigh any cost we may incur. Getting to the truth is our goal. But, if this increases interest and tourism in our state, I couldn't be happier."

FOURTEEN

Beyond the Grave

Only three people were present in Pete Maxwell's bedroom on the night of July 14, 1881, only three witnesses to the single event that has captured the imagination of millions and the attention of historians and enthusiasts for more than a century. One of them was the man alleged to be Billy the Kid, and he was shot down and rendered silent forever. Another was Pete Maxwell, who volunteered little insight on the event during his remaining years. The third was sheriff Pat Garrett, upon whose word the interpretation of what happened that night has been based.

At least two, and more likely three, men were peripheral to what transpired. One was Deputy McKinney, who for years had little to say in public about the event. Another was Deputy Poe, a staunch supporter of and one steadfastly loyal to Garrett, his Masonic brother.

The third witness may have been William Henry Roberts.

Rather than clarify what occurred that fateful night, Garrett's explanations and descriptions, far from being the last word on the subject, have been labeled by scholars as "falsehoods" and over the ensuing decades have led only to confusion, contradiction, and inconsistency, all of which continue to plague serious researchers today.

Why is the Fort Sumner shooting still being questioned today as it was then, questions that began only moments following the shooting? Why is there so little about this single incident and its immediate aftermath that is clear-cut, consistent, and logical? Why has the history of Billy the Kid and his supposed death at the hands of Garrett been so confused and contradictory?

The fact is that the traditional history of Billy the Kid is flawed. It is not so much truth as it is an interpretation of a series of events, mistakes, and deceptions, with most of it based on the Garrett–Upson book. Establishing an accurate history of all aspects of the life and death of Billy the Kid has been, is now, and will likely continue to be difficult. The major problem, according to author Stephen Tatum, arises from the business of separating "history and legend, reality from myth, and truth from fiction." Defining reality as it relates to Billy the Kid is at best problematic. Fact, legend, and misinformation have become so intertwined during the course of the past century that a definitive biography of the true Billy the Kid would be hard to render.

Tatum is correct when he states that to claim anyone is writing reality and truth does not, in and of itself, reveal reality and truth but instead reveals an assertion about reality and truth. This has been a significant and ongoing problem with those who have interpreted and written the history of Billy the Kid, for as human beings, regardless of their stated intentions, they bring to the subject their own personal experiences and perspectives, which often serve to distort their writings.

"The purpose of writing history is to provide a narrative of past events," stated the Roman rhetorician Quintillian. "Since historical events cannot be re-created empirically," according to author Jon Tuska, "they must be re-created by means of a process of inference according to logical principals, ideally taking into account all available evidence." Any historical reconstruction that is "scientific in its determinations and artistic in its formulation," says Morris Cohen in *The Meaning of Human History*, "is the ideal to which professional historians aspire." Tuska further states that what is important in a historical reconstruction of a "former reality" is that it must be undertaken with an understanding "of what the reality was for those who were then living and perceiving it."

According to Tuska, certain questions need to be asked: Is all of the available evidence and pertinent evidence fully taken into account? Are the determinations verifiable by the known historical facts? Are the data reliable? Is the construction based on the documentary evidence logically consistent with the documentary evidence and internally consistent as a construction? How valid are the inferences, and can they withstand logical scrutiny? Are they consistent with all the documentary evidence? "The historian must be willing to admit that this historical reconstruction is at best only probable and provisional, capable of immediate revision in the light of any new evidence which becomes available."

Is all of the available evidence pertinent to Billy the Kid history fully taken into account? The answer is no. In the matter of William Henry Roberts, much of what this enigmatic man has contributed to

Kid history, although stunning in its revelation and accuracy, has largely been resisted by traditionalists.

Even some of the staunchest defenders of the Billy the Kid status quo admit that Roberts possessed an uncanny knowledge of people and events associated with the Lincoln County War. Metz even concedes that a "puzzling fact about Roberts was that, although nearly illiterate, he knew as much about the Lincoln County War as most experts."

The second question—Can the determinations be verified by the known historical data?—provides some problems. In the case of the so-called killing of Billy the Kid, much that is "known" is essentially what Pat Garrett and Ash Upson have chosen to tell. Enlightened Billy the Kid and Lincoln County War scholars are unanimous in their opinions that Garrett and Upson offer little in the way of credibility, yet the contributions of the two via *Authentic Life* are treated as gospel by some. However, a number of Roberts's observations—some prompted, some volunteered, but all firsthand accounts—have held up well under investigation, have been supported by known historical data, and have withstood a barrage of criticism and attack.

The third question concerns the reliability of the data. Data in Billy the Kid history consist for the most part of narrative. Are Roberts's narratives any less reliable or credible than Upson's? Or Garrett's? Based on the evidence, Roberts's credibility may exceed that of Upson and Garrett.

The fourth question is an important one. Is the construction based on the documentary evidence logically consistent with the evidence, and is it internally consistent? With Billy the Kid history, the only possible answer for this is no. The evidence is demonstrably inconsistent and contradictory, and the logic is flawed. However, Roberts's recollections of the Lincoln County War and its related events—including the shooting in Maxwell's room—possess a basic and compelling logic. Roberts's observations often contradict the traditional history but are never internally contradictory. Here was a man, semiliterate, who provided precise descriptions and explanations of events that have eluded credentialed and determined researchers, descriptions and explanations ultimately supported by documentation. The knowledge Roberts possessed could have been obtained only as a result of being a participant.

The fifth and final question poses how valid the inferences are and whether they withstand scrutiny. Concentrated investigation of the traditional published history of Billy the Kid yields more confusion and contradiction than pattern and logic. The deeper one digs into

Roberts's explanations, however, the more one becomes impressed with the consistencies.

An important problem with too many of the traditional Billy the Kid researchers is that they have not been willing to admit that their reconstructions are only probable and provisional and are subject to revision in light of new evidence presented, whether it relates to William Henry Roberts or anything else. Why have individuals resisted the evidence provided by Morrison, Roberts, and others?

Professional researchers steeped in scientific methods tend to be conservative, which is desirable and fitting, for such characteristics inhibit the researchers' immediate acceptance of any and all untested notions. But professionals are generally a prideful lot and do not like to be told they have been mistaken for so long a time. Roberts upset many of them at the outset with his revelations. Many of them may be reluctant to admit that Roberts might have a case because it would be tantamount to admitting that their respective stands and published comments on the topic have been wrong. According to correspondence found in Morrison's files, historians of the 1940s and 1950s, such as Maurice G. Fulton, William Keleher, and Phillip Rasch, were in fact growing receptive to the idea that Roberts was Billy the Kid before they died.

In the case of Billy the Kid, no amount of cloaking the traditional history in the trappings of the research process can hide the fact that it has failed on many points. Intimacy with the history leads to a discomfort with so many loose ends and contradictions. Only careful analysis of Roberts's narratives begins to tie up those loose ends. Very little of what Billy the Kid researchers have claimed over the years relative to the shooting at Maxwell's can be confirmed or substantiated. Speaking of the outlaw Billy the Kid, Frank Richard Prassel writes, "After more than a century of investigation, no one can be certain of his exact name, the details of his birth, or all the facts surrounding his death." In the same vein, Prassel states, "When reduced to proven facts, very little is certain about the Kid's actual life before his arrival in Lincoln County. And much of that which occurred afterward remains controversial and incomplete."

"The whole history of Billy the Kid's life, as it has come down through the years, has been false," writes Ramon Adams in *A Fitting Death for Billy the Kid*. "It has been made up of misstatements of fact, some more consequential than others, but all contributing to the tissue of lies." No matter how hard the traditionalists work to sweep William Henry Roberts under the rug, he continues to intrigue researchers who are interested in the truth. Roberts had detailed knowledge of people, places, and events of the time because he was present. Roberts, an illiterate man, was aware of minute details found only in complicated legal documents filed away in remote collections around the country. An impressive number of Roberts's revelations were never part of the extant publications.

In *Alias Billy the Kid*, Sonnichsen concludes the epilogue by asking the question, "If . . . Roberts wasn't Billy the Kid, then who was he?" If a reader assumes that Roberts was not the Kid, one must still remain impressed, even mystified, by his knowledge of the Lincoln County War, its participants, and pertinent and obscure events. Whether Roberts was the Kid, he must have been there, as Sonnichsen stated, "in the flesh when these things happened." There is no other way to explain how Roberts knew so much.

In spite of the fact that Roberts had no more than the equivalent of a second-grade education, he provided incredible insight into the Lincoln County War and furnished intimate details about events and people missed by historians. Author Stephen Tatum refers to Roberts's revelations as "disturbing" because he "reconstructs certain events in the Kid's life in a manner familiar only to the most devoted Kid researchers." Roberts's story, says Tatum, is a "conceivable effort to confirm the notion that the Kid lived long after 1881."

Roberts's claims are not easily dismissed. If the old man had offered some insight into only one or two events, it could be attributed to coincidence, but there are just too many positive connections, too much accurate detail and insight and substantiated observation to reject his presence and participation in the Lincoln County War and its aftermath.

If Roberts were only seeking publicity, why didn't he stick with the traditionally accepted and oft-reported history of Billy the Kid? Why didn't he claim all of the kills attributed to the Kid? Why didn't he go along with the status quo? It would have been the least demanding route to follow. Instead, Roberts, rather than try to fit himself and his past conveniently into the standard Billy the Kid mold, told what he knew, and what he knew was different from what had long been accepted. The fact is, Roberts's claims were rather modest and unsensational when compared with the established image of Billy the Kid.

Some of the detractors accused Roberts of being a publicity seeker. Roberts never made a dime from his claims and the attendant media coverage. During the last few months of his life, he was talked into signing autographs and appearing with the man who called himself

J. Frank Dalton and claimed to be Jesse James. According to
Morrison's letters, Roberts was extremely uncomfortable with this
activity and after a few experiences vowed never to do it again.

Roberts personally never sought publicity. When confronted with
the charge that he was Billy the Kid, he denied it except to close
friends. When he first met Morrison, he denied he was the Kid.
Roberts never told his wife about his past until after the meeting with
New Mexico governor Thomas Mabry.

Why did Roberts wait until he was almost ninety years of age to reveal his identity? Likely he never would have done so had Morrison
not accidentally discovered him. After all, Roberts, as Billy the Kid,
was a man who believed he was condemned to hang for murder. For
most of his life since July 14, 1881, he was running and hiding from
the hangman's noose. Only after Morrison encouraged that he apply
for a pardon did the true story of his life begin to unfold. In his wan-
ing years, Roberts said that he wanted to "correct some of the lies that
had been told, stop running away, and die a free man."

Who can say for certain whether William Henry Roberts was the
outlaw Billy the Kid? Far too much time has elapsed since the days of
the Lincoln County War, since the shooting in Pete Maxwell's bedroom, and since the death of Roberts on a Hico, Texas, street in 1950
to have absolute proof. All that remains are the words of William
Henry Roberts and Pat Garrett.

Roberts's past, which included the use of a number of aliases and a
lot of moving around, made him difficult to track but not impossible.
Some aspects of his life continue to provide mystery and may always
remain so, but researchers are finding support and verification for his
statements. Thus far, although Roberts has received a barrage of criticism and although his claims have been rejected by some traditionalists, no one has advanced credible proof or evidence that he was an
imposter.

For now, the case for William Henry Roberts as Billy the Kid is far
stronger than the case against it.

Sources

◆◆◆

BOOKS

Adams, Ramon F. *A Fitting Death for Billy the Kid*. Norman: University of Oklahoma Press, 1960.

Ball, Eve. *Ma'am Jones of the Pecos*. Tucson: University of Arizona Press, 1969.

Ball, Larry D. *The United States Marshals of New Mexico and Arizona Territories, 1846–1912*. Albuquerque: University of New Mexico Press, 1978.

Balsiger, David, and Charles E. Sellier Jr. *The Lincoln Conspiracy*. Los Angeles: Schick Sunn Classic Books, 1977.

Bancroft, Hubert Howe. *A History of Arizona and New Mexico, 1530–1888*. San Francisco: History Company, 1889.

Bartholemew, Ed. *Jesse Evans: A Texas Hide-Burner*. Houston: Frontier Press of Texas, 1955.

Bender, Norman J., ed. *Missionaries, Outlaws, and Indians: Taylor F. Ealy at Lincoln and Zuni, 1878–1881*. Albuquerque: University of New Mexico Press, 1984.

Billington, Monroe Lee. *New Mexico's Buffalo Soldiers, 1866–1900*. Niwot: University Press of Colorado, 1991.

Brothers, Mary Hudson. *A Pecos Frontier*. Albuquerque: University of New Mexico Press, 1943.

Burns, Walter Noble. *The Saga of Billy the Kid*. New York: Grosset and Dunlap, 1926.

Clark, Mary Whatley. *John Chisum: Jinglebob King of the Pecos*. Austin, Tex.: Eakin Press, 1984.

Cline, Donald. *Alias, Billy the Kid: The Man Behind the Legend*. Santa Fe, N.M.: Sunstone Press, 1986.

———. *Antrim and Billy*. College Station, Tex.: Creative Publishing, 1990.

Coe, George W. *Frontier Fighter: The Autobiography of George W. Coe*. Boston: Houghton Mifflin, 1934.

Cohen, Morris R. *The Meaning of Human History*. LaSalle, Ill.: Open Court, 1947.

Coolidge, Dane. *Fighting Men of the West*. New York: E. P. Dutton, 1932.

Curry, George. *An Autobiography*. Albuquerque: University of New Mexico Press, 1958.

Dobie, J. Frank. *Some Part of Myself*. Austin: University of Texas Press, 1980.

Dykes, J. C. *Billy the Kid: Biography of a Legend*. Albuquerque: University of New Mexico Press, 1952.

Earle, James H. *The Capture of Billy the Kid*. College Station, Tex.: Creative Publishing, 1989.

Etulain, Richard W., and Glenda Riley. *With Badges and Bullets: Lawmen and Outlaws in the Old West*. Golden, Colo.: Fulcrum, 1999.

Forrester, Izola. *This One Mad Act: The Unknown Story of John Wilkes Booth*. Boston: Hale, Cushman, and Flint, 1937.

Fulton, Maurice G. *History of the Lincoln County War*, edited by Robert N. Mullin. Tucson: University of Arizona Press, 1968.

Garrett, Pat F. *The Authentic Life of Billy the Kid*. Norman: University of Oklahoma Press, 2000. Originally published in 1882.

Gibbon, A. M. *The Life and Death of Colonel Albert Jennings Fountain*. Norman: University of Oklahoma Press, 1965.

Gould, Stephen Jay. *Bully for Brontosaurus*. New York: W. W. Norton, 1991.

Hamlin, William Lee. *The True Story of Billy the Kid*. Caldwell, Idaho: Caxton Printers, 1959.

Hertzog, Peter. *Little Known Facts about Billy the Kid*. Santa Fe, N.M.: Press of the Territorian, 1963.

Hobsbawn, Eric. *Bandits*. New York: Pantheon Press, 1969.

Horn, Calvin. *New Mexico's Troubled Years*. Albuquerque, N.M.: Horn and Wallace, 1963.

Hough, Emerson. *The Story of the Outlaw*. New York: A. L. Burt, 1907.

Hoyt, Henry. *A Frontier Doctor*. New York: Houghton Mifflin, 1929.

Hunt, Frazier. *The Tragic Days of Billy the Kid*. New York: Hastings House, 1956.

Hutchinson, W. H., and Robert N. Mullin. *Whiskey Jim and a Kid Named Billie*. Clarendon, Tex.: Clarendon Press, 1967.

Jameson, W. C. *The Return of the Outlaw, Billy the Kid*. Plano: Republic of Texas Press, 1998.

Kadlec, Robert F. *They Knew Billy the Kid*. Santa Fe, N.M.: Ancient City Press, 1987.

Kaya, Y., and K. Kobayashi. "A Basic Study on Human Faces Recognition." In *Frontiers of Pattern Recognition*, edited by S. Watanabe, 265–89. New York: Academic Press, 1972.

Keleher, William A. *The Fabulous Frontier*. Albuquerque: University of New Mexico Press, 1945.

———. *Turmoil in New Mexico, 1848–1868*. Santa Fe, N.M.: Rydal Press, 1952.

———. *Violence in Lincoln County*. Albuquerque: University of New Mexico Press, 1957.

Knowles, Thomas W., and Joe R. Landsdale. *The West That Was*. New York: Wings Books, 1993.

Koop, Waldo. *Billy the Kid: Trail of a Kansas Legend*. Kansas City, Mo.: Kansas City Westerners, 1965.

Lavash, Donald R. *Sheriff William Brady*. Santa Fe, N.M.: Sunstone Press, 1986.

Lavender, David. *The Southwest*. New York: Harper & Row, 1980.

Leckie, William H. *The Buffalo Soldiers*. Norman: University of Oklahoma Press, 1967.

Mann, E. B. *Guns and Gunfighters*. New York: Bonanza Books, 1975.

McCarty, John L. *Maverick Town: The Story of Old Tascosa*. Norman: University of Oklahoma Press, 1946.

McCright, Grady E., and James H. Powell. *Jesse Evans: Lincoln County Badman*. College Station, Tex.: Creative Publishing, 1983.

Metz, Leon Claire. *Pat Garrett: The Story of a Western Lawman.* Norman: University of Oklahoma Press, 1974.

———. *The Shooters.* El Paso, Tex.: Mangan Books, 1976.

Morrison, John W. *The Life of Billy the Kid: A Juvenile Outlaw.* New York: John W. Morrison, n.d.

Mullin, Robert N., ed. *The Boyhood of Billy the Kid.* Southwestern Studies Monograph 17. El Paso: Texas Western Press, 1967.

———. *A Chronology of the Lincoln County War.* Santa Fe, N.M.: Press of the Territorian, 1966.

———. *Lincoln County War.* Tucson: University of Arizona Press, 1968.

Nolan, Frederick. *The Life and Death of John Henry Tunstall.* Albuquerque: University of New Mexico Press, 1965.

———, ed. *The Lincoln County War.* Norman: University of Oklahoma Press, 1992.

O'Neal, Bill. *Encyclopedia of Western Gunfighter.* Norman: University of Oklahoma Press, 1979.

———. *Henry Brown: The Outlaw Marshal.* College Station, Tex.: Creative Publishing, 1980.

Otero, Miguel. *The Real Billy the Kid: New Light on the Lincoln County War.* New York: Rufus Rockwell Wilson, 1936.

Poe, John W. *The Death of Billy the Kid.* Boston: Houghton Mifflin, 1933.

Pointer, Larry. *In Search of Butch Cassidy.* Norman: University of Oklahoma Press, 1977.

Prassel, Frank Richard. *The Great American Outlaw: A Legacy of Fact and Fiction.* Norman: University of Oklahoma Press, 1993.

Rackocy, Bill. *The Kid.* El Paso, Tex.: Bravo Press, 1985.

Rudulph, Charles Frederick. *Los Billitos: The Story of Billy the Kid and His Gang.* New York: Carlton Press, 1980.

Siringo, Charles A. *A Texas Cowboy; or, Fifteen Years on the Hurricane Deck of a Spanish Pony.* Chicago: M. Umdenstock, 1885.

Sonnichsen, C. L. *I'll Die before I Run: The Story of the Great Feuds of Texas.* New York: Devin-Adair, 1962.

———. *Tularosa: Last of the Frontier West.* Albuquerque: University of New Mexico Press, 1980.

Sonnichsen, C. L., and William V. Morrison. *Alias Billy the Kid.* Albuquerque: University of New Mexico Press, 1955.

Stanley, F. *Dave Rudabaugh: Border Ruffian.* Denver, Colo.: World Press, 1961.

Stedman, Thomas Lathrop. *Medical Dictionary.* Baltimore: Williams and Wilkins, 1976.

Steele, Phillip W., with George Warfel. *The Many Faces of Jesse James.* Gretna, La.: Pelican Publishing Company, 1995.

Tanner, J. M. *Growth at Adolescence.* 2nd ed. Oxford: Blackwell Scientific Publications, 1962.

Tatum, Stephen. *Inventing Billy the Kid.* Albuquerque: University of New Mexico Press, 1982.

Tunstill, William A. *Billy the Kid and Me Were the Same.* Roswell, N.M.: Author, 1988.

Tuska, Jon. *Billy the Kid: A Handbook.* Lincoln: University of Nebraska Press, 1989.

Utley, Robert. *Billy the Kid: A Short and Violent Life*. Lincoln: University of Nebraska Press, 1983.

———. *Four Fighters of Lincoln County*. Albuquerque: University of New Mexico Press, 1986.

———. *High Noon in Lincoln*. Albuquerque: University of New Mexico Press, 1987.

Wallace, Lew. *An Autobiography*. 2 vols. New York: Harper and Bros., 1906.

Wilson, Francis. *John Wilkes Booth: Fact and Fiction of Lincoln's Assassination*. Boston: Houghton Mifflin, 1929.

Wilson, John P. *Merchants, Guns, and Money: The Story of Lincoln County and Its Wars*. Santa Fe: Museum of New Mexico Press, 1987.

ARTICLES

Adler, Alfred. "Billy the Kid: A Case Study in Epic Origins." *Western Folklore* 10 (April 1951): 143–52.

Ball, Eve. "Billy Stikes the Pecos." *New Mexico Folklore Record* 4 (1949–1950): 7–10.

Blazer, Almer. "The Fight at Blazer's Mill in New Mexico." *Frontier Times* (August 1939): 461–66.

Blazer, Paul. "The Fight at Blazer's Mill: A Chapter in the Lincoln County War." *Arizona and the West* 6 (Autumn 1964): 203–10.

Boomersbach, Jana. "Digging Up Billy." *True West* (August–September 2003): 42–45.

Cline, Donald. "Secret Life of Billy the Kid." *True West* (April 1984): 12–17, 63.

Cunningham, Eugene. "I Fought with Billy the Kid." *Frontier Times* (March 1932): 242–47.

DeMattos, Jack. "John Kinney." *Real West* (February 1984): 20–25.

———. "The Search for Billy the Kid's Roots—Is Over!" *Real West* (January 1980): 20–25.

Gomber, Drew. "They Rode with Billy the Kid." *Tombstone Epitaph* (May 2001): 7–10.

Hatley, Allen G. "Old West Adventurer John W. Poe." *True West* (June 1999): 12–18.

Hendron, J. W. "The Old Lincoln County Courthouse." *El Palacio* 46, no. 1 (January 1939): 1–18.

Hutton, Paul. "Billy the Kid as Seen in the Movies." *Frontier Times* (June 1985): 24–29.

Irwin, Helen. "When Billy the Kid Was Brought to Trial." *Frontier Times* (March 1929): 214–15.

Kemp, Ben. "Ride for Mexico, Billy!" *Frontier Times* (March 1980): 6–8.

Kyle, Thomas G. "Computers, Billy the Kid, and Brushy Bill: The Verdict Is In." *True West* (July 1990): 16–19.

Meadows, John P., with Maurice G. Fulton. "Billy the Kid as I Knew Him." Undated manuscripts in the Rasch Collection, Lincoln State Monument, Lincoln, New Mexico.

Metz, Leon. Review of *The Return of the Outlaw, Billy the Kid*. *True West* (September 1998): 52.

Mullin, Robert N. "Here Lies John Kinney." *Journal of Arizona History* 14 (Autumn 1973): 223–42.

Mullin, Robert N., and Charles E. Welch Jr. "Billy the Kid: The Making of a Hero." *Western Folklore* 32 (1973): 104–12.

Nolan, Frederick. "Blazer's Mill: The Gunfight Revisited." *Old West* (Fall 1999): 10–15

———. "Nolan Weighs In." *True West* (April 1999): 5–7.

Rasch, Philip J. "The Bonney Brothers." *Frontier Times* (December–January 1965): 43, 60–61.

———. "The Hunting of Billy the Kid." *English Westerners Brand Book* 11 (January 1969): 1–10.

———. "John Kinney: King of the Rustlers." *English Westerners Brand Book* 4 (October 1961): 10–12.

———. "The Murder of Huston L. Chapman." *Los Angeles Westerners Brand Book* 8 (1959): 69–82.

———. "The Story of Jesse Evans." *Panhandle Plains Historical Review* 33 (1960): 108–21.

———. "War in Lincoln County." *English Westerners Brand Book* 6 (July 1965): 2–4.

Rasch, Philip J., and Robert N. Mullin. "Dim Trails: The Pursuit of the McCarty Family." *New Mexico Folklore Record* 8 (1954): 6–11.

———. "New Light on the Legend of Billy the Kid." *New Mexico Folklore Record* 7 (1952–1953): 1–5.

Sanchez, Lynda. "They Loved Billy the Kid." *True West* (January 1984): 12–16.

Taylor, Leslie. "Facts Regarding the Escape of Billy the Kid." *Frontier Times* (July 1936): 506–13.

Utley, Robert M. "Billy the Kid Country." *American Heritage* (April 1991): 65–78.

Weddle, Jerry. "Apprenticeship of an Outlaw." *Journal of Arizona History* 31, no. 3: 233–52.

NEWSPAPERS

Ashenfelter, S. M. "Exit 'The Kid.'" *Grant County Herald*, July 28, 1881.

Benke, Richard. "NM Lends Support to County's Bid to Verify Billy the Kid Legend." *Albuquerque Journal*, June 10, 2003.

Callon, Milton W. "Las Vegas, New Mexico . . . the Town That Wouldn't Gamble." *Las Vegas Optic*, n.d.

Coe, Frank. "A Friend Comes to the Defense of the Notorious Billy the Kid." *El Paso Times*, September 26, 1923.

El Paso Times. "Researcher Discovers Document." August 5, 1951.

Keck, Benjamin. "Billy the Kid Experts, Fans, to Gather at Symposium." *El Paso Times*, July 23, 1991.

Koogler, J. H. *Las Vegas Gazette*, December 28, 1880.

Las Vegas Gazette. May 19, 1881.

————. December 28, 1881.

Morgan, Art. "Billy the Kid Here Mañana." *Santa Fe New Mexican*, November 29, 1950.

————. "Billy the Kid a Phony It Turns Out." *Santa Fe New Mexican*, November 30, 1950.

Quillen, Ed. "A Grave Way to Attract More Tourists." *Denver Post*, November 16, 2003.

Stallings, Dianne. "Billy the Kid Still Dazzles His Fans." *Ruidoso News*, September 16, 1991.

————. "Tunstill Calls for Showdown over the Kid." *Ruidoso News*, September 8, 1991.

INTERVIEWS

Kuchler, Barbara. Telephone interviews. El Paso, Texas. May 21, 1994; August 17, 1994.

Sonnichsen, C. L. Oklahoma City, Oklahoma. June 25, 1991.

Sweet, Don. Fort Sumner, New Mexico. May 6, 1994.

OTHER

Able, Martile. Notarized affidavit. El Paso County, Texas. August 1, 1950.

Acton, Scott. Unpublished results of computerized pattern-recognition system comparing facial images of William Henry Roberts and Billy the Kid. August 30, 1990.

Bean, Frederic. Transcriptions of taped interviews between William V. Morrison and William Henry Roberts, 1949–1950.

Blazer Papers. Rio Grande Historical Collections, New Mexico State University, Las Cruces.

Gallegos, Severo. Notarized affidavit. Lincoln County, New Mexico. November 11, 1950.

Heath, Martha Vada Roberts. Unpublished genealogical papers.

Lee, Robert E. Notarized affidavit. East Baton Rouge Parish, Louisiana. July 5, 1950.

Montoya, Jose B. Notarized affidavit. Lincoln County, New Mexico. July 3, 1950.

Morrison, William V. "Statement of Facts." November 30, 1950.

Morrison, William V., and C. L. Sonnichsen. Unpublished manuscript containing an account of William Henry Roberts's visit with Governor Thomas Mabry.

Travis, Dewitt. Notarized affidavit. Gregg County, Texas. December 12, 1951.

United States Bureau of Census. 1880 census. Fort Sumner, San Miguel County.

"Who Was Billy the Kid?" *Prime Time Live*. An ABC production aired March 1, 1990.

Index